Learning to Sing

Books published by The Random House Publishing Group
are available at quantity discounts on bulk purchases for
premium, educational, fund-raising, and special sales use.
For details, please call 1-800-733-3000.

Learning to Sing

HEARING THE MUSIC
IN YOUR LIFE

AN INSPIRATIONAL MEMOIR

CLAY AIKEN

WITH ALLISON GLOCK

FAWCETT

BALLANTINE BOOKS • NEW YORK

Although this is a work of nonfiction, some of the names have been changed.

2005 Fawcett Books Mass Market Edition

Published in the United States by Fawcett Books, an imprint of The Random House Publishing Group, a division of Random House, Inc., New York.

FAWCETT BOOKS and colophon are registered trademarks of Random House, Inc.

Originally published in hardcover in the United States by Random House, an imprint of The Random House Publishing Group, a division of Random House, Inc., in 2004.

Grateful acknowledgment is made to Hal Leonard Corporation for permission to reprint "Solitaire," words and music by Neil Sedaka and Phil Cody, copyright © 1972 (Renewed 2000) by EMI Sosasha Music Inc., Songs of SJL-RSL Music Co., EMI Jemaxal Music, Inc., SJL-RSL Songs Co., and Sony/ATV Tunes LLC. All rights for Songs of SJL-RSL Music Co. controlled and administered by EMI Sosasha Music Inc. All rights for SJL-RSL Songs Co. controlled and administered by EMI Jemaxal Music Inc. All rights for Sony/ATV Tunes LLC controlled and administered by Sony/ATV Music Publishing, 8 Music Square West, Nashville, TN 37203. All rights reserved. International Copyright Secured. Used by permission.

All photographs are from the author's collection.

ISBN 0-8129-7410-7

Printed in the United States of America

www.ballantinebooks.com

OPM   9   8   7   6   5   4   3   2   1

For my mother,
who sang to me first

The Lord will fight for you.
All you have to do is stand still.

—Exodus 14:14

CONTENTS

LEARNING TO SING

If you lack purpose you don't touch that many people. And you can touch people through tragedy far better than you can by having a perfect life.

—**Faye Parker, mom**

CHAPTER ONE

Listen First

When I was a kid, the punishment I disliked the most was writing sentences.

My mother loved to make me record my transgressions—always a minimum of five hundred times—and she even bought special spiral notebooks for me to fill up.

"I will not talk back."

"I will not say my dinner is yucky."

"I will not say Granny's face needs ironing."

No matter how many notebooks I went through, there was always another one waiting in the kitchen drawer.

I'm not sure writing sentences stopped me from acting out. But it did make me afraid of writing.

Still, here goes.

—

I wanted to write this book primarily as a thank-you to all the people who have helped me become the man I am. So much has happened since *American Idol,* and in many ways I haven't had an opportunity to reflect. I have toured three times. I have moved twice. I've flown across the country to appear on television programs that I used to watch. I recorded a solo album. A chicken with his head cut off has nothing on me.

My hope is that by writing this book, I will force myself to slow down a little and take the time to savor both the past and the present, to give myself a chance to remember what matters.

I also wanted to share stories about my life in the hope that it might enable a handful of other people to feel better about themselves.

I was dubbed a loser throughout most of my childhood. As a kid, I was an insult magnet—a nerd who loved his grandparents, who wore the wrong clothes, who liked the wrong things, who had goofy hair and glasses, who didn't smoke or drink.

It made for a lonely childhood.

More than a decade later, I figured out that the

real reason people didn't like me was that *I* didn't like me. When I learned to believe in myself, to have faith and to remain stubborn in my convictions, my life changed. Once I decided I was okay, other people agreed. And those folks who didn't agree didn't matter so much anymore.

My mother taught me that we all have the power to achieve our dreams. What I lacked was the courage. The people I write about in this book gave me that courage. I learned from them, and as a former teacher, I believe that lessons should be passed along.

—

Many people think they know me from watching me on television, and in some ways they do. I like to think that what you see is basically who I am.

I like to talk. I'm a terrible dancer. I love my hometown. I have freckles and oversized ears. I'm a geek. I have tried not to hide who I am or what matters to me. Growing up in a friendly Southern town, I wasn't trained for subterfuge. My mama believed in honesty and integrity, and I have endeavored to live up to her example.

No person matures by himself. We have all had someone who reached down and picked us up when we couldn't manage to rise on our own. We have all been carried. I know I have been.

I was blessed with a mother who is strong, smart,

and filled with the sort of decency that is out of fashion these days. Her fortitude enabled me to rise above circumstances that otherwise would have crushed me.

"*Que será, será,*" she would sing to me every night as I drifted off to sleep. "Whatever will be, will be."

Mom helped me to see that every person is like a painting. When you come into contact with another life, that individual dabs a little bit of color onto your soul. It isn't always a color you like, but even ugliness provides its own lessons.

I learned this the hard way. There was no shortage of ugliness in my childhood. My daddy drank too much, and when he did, he turned to violence. Mom and I spent much of my early childhood disentangling ourselves from him.

Then I went to grade school and discovered a whole new form of cruelty: the heartlessness of exclusion.

Pain happens to everyone. To grow up, to fulfill your potential, to develop into what God wants you to be—this process takes support. No one succeeds alone.

It is like making an album. I may sing, but someone else writes the songs, someone produces, another person engineers, another person packages, another person markets, another person sells it, another person buys it. To say I created a platinum-selling album is silly. A group created it. Life is collaboration.

Now, I'm able to screw things up on my own; that's not a problem. But getting things right—that takes assistance and guidance.

—

I believe God has a plan. God has a direction for me. He may put me on a few detours, but the path will ultimately reveal itself. My job is to be a decent human being no matter how rocky the road gets.

Lately, the road has been pretty bumpy. Adjusting to life in Hollywood, far from the comfort of home, has been a challenge. I have had to adapt to so many things. Distance from my family. Traffic. Avocado on all the food.

Most of my new life is amazing. But then there are times when I look around and notice that everyone around me is a stranger. In Raleigh, I had friends for eighteen years. Out in L.A., I spend my days around people who have been in my world for only three months. I may see them every day, but they don't know me.

—

When I taped the *Primetime Live* interview with Diane Sawyer, I was struck for the first time with how significantly my life had changed. We were setting up in an old nightclub in New York City. There were arches, banquettes, and a curtained stage. The floor was checkered. It reminded me of the sort of place where Sinatra might have performed.

When I arrived, there were bright lights and cameras everywhere. People scurried around with clipboards and cell phones. There were producers and management teams and makeup artists and wardrobe consultants and camera operators and lighting experts and caterers and assistants for the assistants. I was stuck in the corner and I watched these masses of people rushing and bustling because of me. I wondered: *Why?* What had I really done? I sang. But I had always sung. Suddenly, people cared.

Since then, my entire circle of friends has changed. The people I thought would always be my peers really aren't anymore.

—

I used to imagine what a typical day would be like once I grew up. I thought maybe I'd have a crappy time at work and I would call my friends who were also teachers and ask their advice about how to reach a particular student. Then I'd drive home or maybe meet my family for dinner at Applebee's.

Now it seems all my new friends are people who work for me. And when I don't have a job for them, they may not be around.

There are many days when I consider quitting. I fantasize about trading places with buddies who are teaching back in North Carolina, leading the life I thought would be mine.

I relished being in the classroom. My whole existence had been mapped out down to the career conflict I would have: Would I want to be a principal or stay a teacher? Would I move to a high school or continue teaching elementary-level special ed?

When my friends back home tell me stories about connecting with children, I feel acutely that I'm not making a difference. I find it difficult to believe that my getting more famous helps anyone else.

Some days it would be nice to forget it all happened and go to the mall. When I feel down like that, I try to focus on what is good about my life now.

I am making more money for charity than I ever would have been able to earn as a teacher. I have a broader platform for calling attention to children with special needs.

I am singing.

—

To me, singing is the single most joyous thing a person can do.

A song is like a smile. If you meet someone from another country, even if you don't speak the same language, you know what a smile means. A song works the same way. Music produces feelings that need no translation.

My mother prophesied years ago that my voice would take me places. She was certain that there was a reason I was able to sing. I am still discovering what that reason is. I am only twenty-five. I still have many unanswered questions.

I've had to learn that whatever comes out of this is what God wants to happen. The challenge now is to find a way to do good work.

American celebrities have an amazing amount of influence on the way young people in our country think, feel, and act. I believe that such influence should be used in the most constructive way possible. I want to use my voice to inspire good in others. I never want to produce anything that a family could not enjoy together. I never want to create art that would embarrass my own children later.

I do this because it feels right.

I do this because if I didn't, my mother would snatch me bald-headed.

As she should.

One Sunday afternoon I decided to stay home with Clayton instead of going to my mother's house. He must have been around two and a half. It was a mistake because I became so blue during the day. I found myself sitting on the sofa looking out the window. The stereo was playing some sad music and the depression finally overcame me. Clayton, being such a sensitive child, noticed and said, "Mama, what you thinking about?"

"Oh, a lot of things," I said.

"Mama, you got cry in your eyes. What you need? You need me?"

I told him the music was making me sad.

"Okay," he said. "You come to my room and I'll play you some happy music."

And he took me upstairs and sat me down and started to sing for me.

—**Faye Parker**

CHAPTER TWO

Decide What Song You Want to Sing

I *am a mama's boy.*

When I was three years old, my mother lifted me from the tub and I kicked the edge. I started crying, and she said, "It'll get well before you're married."

I wasn't sure what married was, so I asked. She replied that a wife was someone who would cook for me and wash my clothes and love me, and I said to her, "I'm already married."

Mom laughed and said, "To whom?"

And I said, "You, Mama!"

—

I was born Clayton Holmes Grissom on November 30, 1978, in the Rex Hospital in Raleigh, North Carolina. I weighed six pounds, eleven ounces, and already had a thatch of red hair. I also was born with a collapsed lung.

After I was delivered, I was immediately put on a respirator, and a tube was inserted into my chest to help me breathe. My mother wept. My birth father, Vernon, left the hospital and went to the parking lot to get drunk. This was something he did often, and having a sick baby was a better excuse than most.

When I was a bit older, my mother confessed to me that she had not especially wanted a child. She knew Vernon was an alcoholic, knew also what happened after he drank too much, when he got angry and decided she was the reason for his pain. She did not desire to bring a baby into the chaos and violence of her life and wondered why God had seen to make her pregnant at such a dark time.

Her pregnancy was rough, and she did not look forward to my birth. She was unable, as she explains it, to bond with me, to celebrate my arrival. But I came anyway, and she says that at the moment she heard me wailing, she fell instantly in love.

—

From the day of my birth on, my mother and I were inseparable. Predictably, the addition of an infant did not improve circumstances at home. Vernon did not rise to the occasion.

Before I turned three years old, we left him. We moved out with only the clothes on our backs and took refuge at the home of Mom's friend from work, Amaryllis McGhee, a woman whom I call Nanny and think of as a second grandmother. We slept on a mattress in Nanny's living room, between the front door and the kitchen. She hung a tarp around the bed so we'd have privacy.

The first night we were there, Vernon threatened to come and start trouble, so Mama went to the police station to get a restraining order. By the time she arrived, he had already been arrested for public drunkenness.

Ours was not an ideal situation, but my mother made it work. I know it was a struggle, but she kept from me just how difficult it really was. I was never told how bad our money problems were or how depressed she may have felt. She protected me not only from my birth father but from as many harsh realities as she could. More often than not, she distracted me with music.

—

My mother drove a yellow Ford Torino.

Day care was expensive, so Mama took me with her as many places as she could, including Sears, where she worked as a decorating consultant in the wall hanging department. When she couldn't keep me at Sears, she'd drive me to Nanny's house or an hour outside of Raleigh to Granny Aiken's farm.

Mom preferred country music to any other type, so by age four I had memorized quite a few hillbilly tunes. I remember the two of us singing together in the car, passing the time while we drove wherever we were going.

Around that time, Mom took Granny and me to the Grand Ole Opry. We were touring the stage and one of the people working there asked whether anybody in the group wanted to come up and sing. Mom says I was on that stage quicker than you could drop a bucket.

I sang, "Mammas Don't Let Your Babies Grow Up to Be Cowboys." Everyone laughed and clapped. I don't think it was that I was particularly good, just that I was little and loud. If a kid climbs onstage and sings, you're going to applaud.

Clearly, I wasn't afraid of performing, but I was frightened of everything else. I was a skittish child. I didn't like bugs or loud noises. When my mom would go to the bathroom, I would hide behind the couch. I didn't like to be separated from her—not even for a few minutes. I'm sure it had something to do with our history of taking cover from my birth father. I had this idea that I could be snatched away at any time, and leaving my mama was the last thing I wanted.

I remember one afternoon I was taking a nap and I woke up in a sweat, afraid I was going to have to go to Vernon's house. He and I had scheduled visitation every other week. Nothing bad ever happened there, but the idea of being away from Mom's side sent me into a panic.

For years, Mom worked Thursday nights at Sears. Even though the routine was identical every week, even though I knew it was coming, I cried when she had to leave. I never got used to seeing her walk out the door.

—

Maybe because of all the crying and clinging, Mom worried that as a single parent she wasn't providing me with enough masculine activities. So when I was old enough, she enrolled me in T-ball.

It was a disaster. I was without question the worst T-ball player Raleigh had ever seen. Even my mother was forced to concede that I was terrible, and she never thought anything I did was short of breathtaking.

I loathed T-ball. I stunk at T-ball. But when the season ended, I signed up for the next year. I played because I thought my mom wanted me to. I didn't want to disappoint her. I was willing to struggle through it, but if I remember right, Mom spared me a second season of humiliation and suggested I take piano lessons instead.

———

My piano teacher, Sandra Powell, was in her early forties, and we had lessons at her house.

I hated the piano. I was a poor student, and so after about two months of banging on the keys, Mom said, "Why don't we see if we can get her to teach voice?"

Now, Sandra was one loud woman. Her house was filled with all sorts of clutter and antiques. Lots of crushed velvet. Lots of precious stuff stacked in cabinets. When she sang, pieces of glass would rattle. The only way I could hear myself was if I sang as loud as I could, because this woman had some lungs on her. She may not have taught me how to sing, but she did teach me how to project.

I liked Sandra, but I hated having to practice. So, typically stubborn, I refused to. And my mom, never one to waste money, said, "If you're not going to try, then you're not going to go." And that was the end of my voice lessons. I think I lasted for about two months.

This is why, when people ask how I learned to sing, I always credit my mother. Because those hours driving in the Ford Torino were far more influential than any lessons or the church choir. I may have picked up the formalities of music from those places, but the true spirit of singing came from listening to my mom warble Patsy Cline songs as we drove through the North Carolina countryside.

Her voice wasn't trained, but it was beautiful. It made me feel things. It showed me how a song can be more than words and music, how when sung with soul a song carries you to another world, to a place where no matter how much pain you feel, you are never alone.

—

When I was six, my mother remarried. Her new husband was one of her coworkers at Sears, a man named Ray Parker. A year later, she had my brother, Brett. Mom wasn't sure about enduring another pregnancy at her age, but Ray was so keen to try that she consented.

We all lived together in a modest, blue two-story house in Raleigh with a big garage and a fenced backyard. Ray had been married before and had a son, Jeff, and a daughter, Amy, who visited on occasion, usually at Christmastime.

Mom would always warn us, "You're going to be disappointed this year."

She didn't want us to get our hopes up about the gifts, because we didn't have as much spending money as the other kids.

I remember asking for a phone for my room.

"You're going to be so let down," Mom said.

"We're not going to be able to give you every-thing."

And then, like a Christmas miracle, the box I unwrapped contained a phone. Now, it was the cheapest, made-in-Japan, on-the-damaged-box-shelf-at-Wal-Mart phone—but it was a phone. I don't know how she managed to find the money, but she did.

Thus, she expected us to appreciate every gift we received. One year I got a model of a spaceship, a shuttle that you put together on your own. I un-wrapped it and said, "Thank you, thank you very much," but in truth I was not a model-shuttle-building type of guy. Nintendo-playing, maybe. But a model? That was a little too labor-intensive for me. So I stuck it in my closet.

The next Christmas, I was opening my gifts and my main present was another model shuttle.

"Mom, you got me one just like this last year," I whined.

And she said, "No. I got you that one. You never opened it. So don't tell me you never get stuff, be-cause if you have enough toys to leave one un-opened, then you have more than enough."

—

During the holidays it doesn't snow much in Raleigh, but occasionally an inch or two will fall. Whenever it snowed when I was young, my mom and I made snow cream. We ran outside and scraped the snow off the hood of the car and then mixed it with sugar and milk and ate the result.

Mom would also take me out in the cold to pull taffy. She would make the batter and then we would yank and grab at it until it got stiff enough to put into candies.

I was twelve years old, and she would be jerking, yanking, pulling on this wad of taffy, shouting, "Pull harder, Clayton, come on!" I hated it at the time, but when I look back now, I would give anything to go home and pull some taffy. I was the only one Mom asked to help her, and I see today that it was her way of spending some time alone with me.

Most of my memories of her are like that. Simply her being there, either sitting, smiling, in the audience when I would sing, or standing in the winter air eating snow cream.

I remember one holiday, all I got for Christmas was batteries. Batteries are expensive, and I had complained all year about never having enough. Mom shut me up about that.

Another season, I begged for a VCR. Now, this was something my mom saw no point in allowing me to have. She said if I really wanted one, I'd have to buy it myself.

So I did. I saved the money I was making by mowing yards and bagging groceries and bought myself a VCR. I could not have enjoyed that VCR more. I used to wash the thing.

I learned—which is, I'm sure, what my mother intended—that when you buy your own things, you take care of them a lot better. When something is earned, it pays dividends far greater than when something comes easy.

When I was growing up, Mom took care that everything on the surface looked okay. She hid how poor we really were. My mom never bought name-brand anything. I never wore Nikes or Reeboks. I had Roos.

Actually, I don't even think I had them. I think most of my shoes didn't even have a name on them. Canvas and rubber, that's what they were.

But my feet never got wet, just the same.

We did purchase things, but we always got them five years after they came out because we were waiting for the prices to go down. And we tended to buy off-brand stuff—for instance, I think our answering machine was gas-powered.

Basically, we got by. We did what we needed to do. Mom and Dad were frugal almost to the point of being cheap. But we survived plenty well.

"You don't need to be rich to be happy," Mom said. "Look at Leona Helmsley. She's rich and she's miserable."

Mom thought that craving designer shoes, video games, and CD players obscured what really counted. "Owning *things* doesn't teach you anything about life," she'd say. "Food. Shelter. That's what priorities should be."

This was not an easy lesson for a kid—especially once I reached high school, where labels of all kinds dominate.

I remember Mom used to proudly walk in and out of the discount shoe store. And I used to be so embarrassed that I wouldn't carry the bag. Mom would say, "Fine, I'll carry it. Poverty is no reason for shame."

When we shopped at the thrift store, I would whine, "Why aren't we at Abercrombie & Fitch?"

My mother would shake her head and say, "What you wear doesn't matter. Who you *are* does."

—

My mother has always had the highest hopes for both my younger brother, Brett, and me.

She was very strict about how her children presented themselves to the world. She wanted to be certain that we were upstanding citizens, honest and honorable, and that we were never intentionally unkind.

"To handle yourself, use your head," she'd say. "To handle others, use your heart."

—

My father used to own rental property, trailers mostly, that he would let out for extra income. One tenant was having difficulty making his payments. Dad wanted to evict him, but Mom said no.

"You should always be willing to work with someone who's willing to help themselves," she said.

The rest of the family thought this guy was a loser. But Mom refused to abandon him, so instead of evicting him she gave him a job painting the house. When it was done she wiped away his debt.

That was the example she set for me: Give people a chance to be the best they can. Think well of someone and see if they rise to the occasion.

—

Now that I'm older, I may see her point more often, but my mama and I still fight all the time.

This, I believe, is a good thing. You fight with the people you love the most. You don't fight with people you don't trust or respect—or whom you barely know. Those people may up and leave and never let you have the chance to win the argument. You could actually alienate them if you pick a fight.

But your family, they have to stick around. And your mama, she has to love you no matter what. I have spent my life taking full advantage of that fact.

Mostly, we bicker. I don't think I can recall a conversation with her on the phone when I didn't argue with her or upset her. We have high expectations of each other, and that can lead to disputes.

I don't think our relationship is that much different from many other people's relationships with their mothers.

She is a mom, she nags me.

She expects nothing but the best from me.

She brags about me as if she has to, because she sort of *does* have to, I guess.

What's different about the relationship between my mother and me is that we share such a binding history. Not that other people aren't close to their moms, but the two of us have been through a whole bunch of bad stuff together. We were all the other person had for a long while.

What we quarrel about is never anything horribly important.

Mom: You never call enough.

Me: I'm busy.

Mom: I never get enough time with you.

Me: I'm not a child anymore, Mom.

Mom: You're not so big I can't throw you across my knee.

Me: Actually, I am.

Mom: Don't sass me, boy.

Me: I'm not a boy!

—

I will forever be trying to be the man my mother expects me to be.

She remains an uncompromising presence in my world. When she comes to my shows and sits in the audience, I get nervous. She is the only person who can do that to me. Even at twenty-five years old, I'm still trying to impress her—the way I did when we sang together in the car, the way I did in T-ball, the way I did in school and in church.

When Brett went off to the Marines, I was on vacation in London. Mom phoned me, and she was crying.

I tried to comfort her, but it wasn't working. I realized that it was the first time I had ever heard my mother cry for herself. She'd cried for me plenty. And for Brett.

Whenever we were hurting, she cried. She worried about Papa getting sick, and she cried. She worried about Granny being alone, and she cried. But she never felt pity for herself.

The day she phoned she was out of control.

I asked what I could do. I wanted to be a rock for my mother. She'd had enough tragedy in her life. She was abused physically, emotionally, and mentally. And she dealt with it. She weathered her trials and grew stronger through the experiences. She's the queen of lemonade making, in my opinion. She goes through BS and comes out smelling like a rose.

"Mom, stop crying. Please," I begged.

And she said, "Just let me weep. I'm allowed to be upset, I'm allowed to *be*."

She reminded me that within a period of two years her husband had died, one son had left home for

Hollywood, and the other had joined the Marines, and that maybe that warranted a good cry.

When Mom said that, I felt more like a man than I ever had, because she trusted that I could handle the truth. She believed I could take it. She could finally allow herself to hurt in front of me.

I no longer needed to be protected. I was grown.

—

I was the musical guest on *Saturday Night Live* in February 2004.

After the show, the cast always hosts a party at a bar. Now, generally, I avoid bars. I don't drink. I hate smoke. I can't stand to have to shout at my friends over a bunch of noise. I'm afraid of crowds. The only reason people go to bars is to get drunk and have sex. To me, bars are what hell is like. But I decided if I was ever going to be in a bar, the night I got to be on *Saturday Night Live* would be the time to go.

While I was there, a friend dared me to have a cocktail. She had ordered a Cosmopolitan, and when it came I asked her what it was.

"Delicious," she told me. "Try it."

I refused. Alcohol doesn't interest me much.

"I bet you can't drink it," she chided.

Now, I'm old enough to know when I'm being manipulated. But it had been a huge night for me.

Appearing on the show had been a longtime dream of mine, and it had gone exceptionally well.

"Go on," she urged, pushing the drink in my face.

So I did. I drank the whole thing in one gulp.

All my friends at the party were stunned. They had never seen me drink before, not even a sip of beer. People cheered and applauded. I was feeling pretty proud of myself. And then I felt my face get really, really hot.

Now, not having ever been drunk, I didn't really know what drunk felt like. I did know that I was growing dizzy and that my face felt like it was on fire. I decided I had better find a seat. It was at that moment that *SNL* creator Lorne Michaels walked up and introduced himself.

"Hello," he said, "I'm Lorne."

I started trembling. I wondered if he could smell alcohol on my breath. My mind was racing.

"Would you like to sit down?" he asked.

Why was he asking me to sit down? Did he think I needed to sit down? Did he think I was drunk? *Was* I drunk?

"The show was terrific," he said.

I don't remember what I said.

"Well, Clay, a pleasure to meet you."

I don't remember what I said then, either.

Lorne walked away, and I heard my mother's voice in my head. *What were you thinking, Clayton? Who are you trying to impress? When success turns a person's head, he is facing failure.*

It was true, of course. Even through the fog of a Cosmopolitan, I knew Mama was right.

—

It's no surprise to me that it's my mother's words I hear in my head. Other people call it a conscience. I call it Mom.

There were a number of times when I might've given in to something if it hadn't been for her voice telling me to stand firm.

"A clean conscience is a soft pillow," she'd say. "As long as you live right, you won't have to worry about what people see."

I never smoked or drank, and I know that was because I could hear her saying that those habits were nasty and weak—and because if I were caught, I knew she would look down on me, and that was deterrent enough.

I always wanted to make my mama happy.

I think it's because when we left my birth father, she was terrified and alone. I sensed that she needed something to keep her going. I decided that something would be me.

From the time I was a boy, Mama would talk to me about what sort of man I was planning to become. "What kind of person do you aspire to be? What do you think matters?" she would ask. If I answered selfishly, she'd correct me, either with words or by example.

—

When she was younger, my mom wanted to be a singer. She sang in a bunch of what she called "rinky-dink country bands." One was named the Rustic Spirits. She was the lead vocalist, and my birth father played guitar.

Mom says she was never very good, but that she was "petite and vivacious." She performed in high heels and a big Loretta Lynn wig. She sang for ten years. Then I was born, and that was the end of that.

Instead of being a singer, she became the sole guardian of my innocence. She kept the darkness at bay. It was her sacrifices that enabled me to have a childhood, her unbreakable optimism that infused hope into my life.

Mother says she has never regretted giving up on her ambition to sing professionally. And I believe her.

"Life is a dance you learn as you go," she says with a shrug.

But I do think about her voice sometimes when I am singing. How she used to hum me a lullaby at bedtime. "Que Será, Será." "My Little Buckaroo."

Now I am the one singing to her. I hope she likes what she hears.

Blood isn't always thicker than water.

—Faye Parker

CHAPTER THREE

Understand the Importance of a Good Band

My great-granddaddy Joseph Aiken was a musician. He played fiddle, banjo, and other down-home instruments.

He was written up in the Raleigh *News & Observer* in 1967, when he was seventy-six years old. They even ran a photograph of him picking, calling him "a master fiddler."

He was part of a Duke University preservation project. His songs were recorded and are now kept in the Library of Congress as a portion of a folk culture archive. The selections include "What a Friend We Have in Jesus" and "Intoxicated Rat."

His brother Romie Aiken is also in the archive.

His songlist offers "If the Ocean Was Whiskey and I Was a Duck, I'd Dive to the Bottom and Never Come Up."

I feel I have these men to thank not only for my musical leanings but also for my sense of humor.

—

I come from a big family.

Not big in the traditional sense. My immediate family consists of me, my mother, and my brother, Brett. But our extended family is huge. My granny is the twelfth of thirteen surviving children, seventeen kids in all. Obviously, her parents didn't have a TV.

My grandparents in my mother's family are Alvis Aiken and Catherine Clayton, which is where I got my name. It's a Southern tradition to be given your first name from your grandmama's maiden name.

My middle name came from my paternal grandmother's maiden name, which is Holmes. And then, obviously, the last name initially came from my birth father, until I changed it to Aiken.

Granny and Papa Aiken had three kids. My mother is the oldest. My Uncle Don is two years younger than she is, while my Uncle Jerry is seven years younger. All of them have been married twice, which seems to be another family tradition.

In Uncle Don's first marriage he had a son, Donald Aiken Jr. And then he married my mother's best friend from high school, Lelia. So my mom's best friend became her sister-in-law, which was kind of nice. Lelia already had two kids, Cyndi and Danny, from her first marriage.

I don't know anything about Uncle Jerry's first marriage, I do know that he's married to Dianne Taylor now and they have two kids, Jessica and Lee.

My birth father, Vernon, has one younger sister, Mary Helen, but everybody just calls her Mer Helen. His first marriage produced one child, my half sister, Deb. Deb had two kids, Jeffrey and Casey; one is a month older than me and one is two years younger. Then Aunt Mer Helen has two kids, Jimmy and Bobby, in that order.

My stepfather was the youngest of six. His brother Willie Earl died when I was twelve. He was married to Shirley Parker, and they have three kids, Ricky, Felix, and Karen.

The next in line is Christine. She's the one who has kind of become the matriarch of the family. She's the oldest daughter, and she's as old as, if not older than, my grandmother. She has four kids, Vernon, Sharon, Terry, and Marty. And they all have kids that are my age. So all of my second cousins are really the ones I treat as my cousins. My first cousins I treat as my aunts and uncles. And my aunt I treat like my grandmother.

Confused yet?

Uncle Wilton is married to Shirley. They have five boys, Randy, Gary, Keith, Alan, and Chris. And they all have families of their own. Uncle Gerald is married to Aunt Mamie. Aunt Lois is married to Uncle James, and they've got four kids, Kim, Beverly, Kevin, and Tamara. And they all have families, too.

And then my stepdad married Mom, and there you go.

Whew!

—

In addition to all of my relatives, there are the McGhees.

Though she was considerably older, Amaryllis McGhee was my mother's best friend from Sears. The two of them were the cutups of the place. Well, Amaryllis was a cutup and my mama laughed along.

It was to Amaryllis's house that my mother ran the night we escaped from my birth father. And it was in her house that we stayed for months, setting up in her living room by the front door, refugees from a ruined life.

Even after Mom got back on her feet and we found a little house of our own, I still visited Amaryllis every week. Over time, she became a second grandmother to me. I began to call her Nanny. Her husband, Roscoe, became Pop.

Nanny looked after me when I wasn't at the babysitter's or at my other granny's house in the country. And it was Nanny who introduced Mom to her second husband, Ray Parker. Ray also worked at Sears, in the home improvement department. Apparently, he won my mother over when he left a box of chocolates on her chair on Valentine's Day. Nanny thought it was a little cowardly of him not to just ask her out directly, but she didn't hold it against him.

———

Nanny and Pop lived by the fairgrounds. There was a train station there, and each time I heard a train coming, Nanny and Pop would walk me down so I could watch it pass. We'd put pennies on the track to be flattened, and we'd yell into the noise as the engine screeched by.

When I was a child, Nanny and I watched the ball drop in Times Square on the television in her bedroom every New Year's Eve. The two of us would sit on the bed, keeping each other awake until midnight. Pop always fell asleep too soon. But no matter how exhausted she was, Nanny stayed up.

Once the ball dropped, we would cheer and sing "Auld Lang Syne." Nanny always made the holiday a big deal. After celebrating, I would snuggle under the blankets and drift off to sleep with my head on her shoulder. I did this every year, even after I had grown old enough to be invited to more traditional parties.

—

I loved the feeling I had when I was at Nanny and Pop's place. There was a different social dynamic with the McGhees than with the Aikens. Their family was boisterous and loud, whereas the Aikens were soft-spoken and nonconfrontational.

At the Aikens' we'd sit around quietly and chat about benign topics. Maybe we'd go outside for a swing in the backyard. At home, I was forever being told to "hush up."

But at Nanny and Pop's, everybody had a big mouth. They'd talk, talk, talk, and talk. You had to fight for airtime. Nanny alone could talk your ear off. She could talk until it bled when you left.

She knew everyone in Raleigh—and Raleigh ain't too small. She knew them all, and she knew their children, too. Once Nanny met you, she remembered you for the rest of her life. She had a mind like a steel trap. I recall being amazed that as much as she talked, she was still able to listen.

The other thing that amazed me was how messy she was. You had to swim through her dining room. She wouldn't throw anything away. Wrapping paper, pictures, grocery bags. She'd just stack her stuff on top of something else until it became a tower. Then she'd start another one right beside it.

It seemed that at the McGhees' there was always a party going on. The scene in the house was rowdy and bawdy. Lots of jokes were told. I'd have to say that I remember my birthday parties there more vividly than I do the ones at Granny's.

I recall that on my third birthday there were a ton of people in the kitchen and everyone wanted to hug on me. I can visualize the candles on the cake and a raucous crowd of people singing "Happy Birthday," then "ooohhhhing" when I blew the candles out. There were balloons and noisemakers. I felt like a king. I can still see the bright pop of what seemed like a hundred flashbulbs going off.

Nanny is the same age as Granny, but to me she never seemed quite as old. She moved around with no problem. She traveled, taking bus trips with groups of seniors. As a kid, she had felt like a city person, even though she wasn't. They had a farm and grew collards in the backyard, but still they managed to come off as urban.

I remember taking vacations with them, and we'd go to the beach with her granddaughters, Yvonne and Yvette. We'd all be horsing around, splashing and building castles, and there Nanny would be in her swimsuit and sunscreen and giant Jackie O glasses, wanting to be a part of everything.

Sometimes she'd take me to a theme park and dare me to ride the roller coasters. I was too timid, of course.

—

What I learned from Nanny and Pop, and their children, and all the folks who came to our aid in those difficult times, is that family is what you make it. Family is about love.

Even now, I regard the McGhees as my grandparents. I call Nanny's children Aunt Donna and Aunt Joan. We celebrate Christmas together.

I view Granny and Nanny as peers. They do, too. They treat each other like family—which is what they are.

—

Unlike Nanny, Granny Aiken was not into theme parks.

She grew up in the country, and like every child reared in the country, Granny was a worker. She helped till the fields, and she pulled potatoes. She knew how to paint a house and mend a fence. To make money, her family sold tomatoes, okra, and other vegetables at roadside stands. Being part of a family of fifteen, she had a necessarily meager existence during her upbringing.

The whole family stayed close. Even after they'd grown up, nobody moved outside a ten-mile radius of the farm.

I can never remember my granny not doing something. When I stayed with her on the weekends, while Mom worked overtime at Sears, Granny put me to work. I yanked carrots out of the ground. I beat rugs. I scrubbed sinks. I snapped peas. I battled weeds. I tilled the soil. We sat out in the backyard with a little metal wash tin and snapped the ends off pole beans for hours. I hated it.

The only time Granny ever took a break was to watch her stories. She would go inside to the living room, turn on the TV, and settle in with her soap operas. If I stayed quiet while she watched, I was allowed to turn on *Sesame Street* after the soap ended. I lay on the floor in the middle of the room while she sat in her chair. Papa would be asleep on the couch.

I usually dozed off and awoke to the sound of the *Sesame Street* theme song. Granny would have changed the channel and already left the room to do more chores. She gave herself an hour to rest and felt it was more than enough.

I can't say that as a boy I thought it was a great time to snap beans and scrub pots, but I do remember how at home I felt at Granny's house. I loved the way it smelled in the country—sweet and thick, the scent of overgrowth and vegetation run wild.

Hard work is not a value you enjoy as you acquire it. But it is a value you come to appreciate later—and to disdain the absence of in others.

—

In addition to the farming, Granny worked a second job at my mom's old high school, running the cash register in the cafeteria.

I remember being up there one day when I was three or four. Granny sat me on her lap and let me work the machine with her. She told me which buttons to push, and all the kids thought it was so cute, until I hit the wrong key and the cash register locked up.

In no time, a long line of chippy high schoolers formed. "What's the holdup?" they asked, shuffling their feet and rebalancing their trays.

Granny beat on the machine, pushing buttons as quickly as she could. Nothing worked. The machine stayed quiet.

I was certain that I was going to get Granny fired. I began to cry. But Granny didn't panic. She just said, "I swanee," and plucked away at the register until it finally popped open.

She was tolerant in that way. Granny was not a wimp or a complainer, and she didn't much care for people who were. She was also known to be stubborn. That's a Clayton family trait. We're stubborn and feisty.

My mom said Granny was the disciplinarian at the Aiken house. She was firm but fair. I recall that she didn't have a problem snapping me into shape when I was a kid. I remember her saying "For crying out loud" so many times, it felt like my first name.

Granny may have been resolute and industrious, but when it counted, she was able to laugh at herself.

One time when we were at my uncle's house, Dad told this joke about two teenagers cruising along on a date when all of a sudden the guy driving the car pulls over and tells his date that he's run out of gas. The punchline was along the lines of "If you ain't here after what I'm here after you're going to be here after I'm gone."

Granny listened, but she didn't laugh. She sat there for a minute, then asked, "Well did he get the gas or not?"

Oh, did we all make fun of her for that. From then on, every time she didn't get a joke, Dad would say, "Did you get the gas, Granny?" And she would giggle like a young girl. Granny was never afraid to laugh at herself, which is a noble quality, I think.

—

Days at Granny's house were largely a drag. But the evenings were more fun.

At dinner, the food was unbeatable. Fried chicken and gravy. Fresh corn dripping in butter. Ripe slices of watermelon pooling juice on the plate. Homemade peanut butter pie and icy cold milk.

Every night after dinner Papa fell asleep listening to the Grand Ole Opry. He would turn in early, going to his bedroom around nine, when the program started.

Sometimes I'd go in there and lie down with him

and listen to the music coming from his tiny radio. It was country and bluegrass, the music my mother loved and sang to me in the car. I was allowed to stay with Papa as long as I was peaceful. If I recognized the tune, I could sing along quietly, but that was it.

He didn't want anybody interrupting his Grand Ole Opry. He said that listening to that music was the best part of his day.

—

My papa has Alzheimer's now. When we see each other, his eyes widen with recognition, but he has trouble saying the words. We hug instead, and he doesn't let go for a long time.

Granny says he can't remember much about his past and has difficulty processing the present. But he does ask about me. And if I happen to be on TV at night, he'll sit up and watch, no matter how late.

Recently Granny told me that Papa doesn't listen to the Grand Ole Opry at bedtime anymore. He listens to my CD. Every night she asks if he might like to hear something different, but he refuses. Instead, he puts in my music and pushes "play."

It's as if I am still there, like I was as a child, lying beside him and singing him to sleep as the darkness falls.

—

I've often wondered how Granny and Papa must feel about Nanny and Pop—whether they have ever been jealous. There have been times when it would have been perfectly reasonable for Granny's feelings to be hurt, for her to feel upstaged. But she has never expressed even a whiff of resentment. I can only imagine that the trial Mom and I went through must have bonded Nanny and Granny deeply.

I remember that on the night Brett was born I slept over at Nanny's house because she and Pop lived right by the hospital. The next morning we went to visit.

After I saw Brett, Dad led me out to the waiting area where both Nanny and Granny were sitting. He told me I was allowed to bring one person back with me to see the baby.

I stood frozen, eyeing Nanny and Granny, terrified. How could I choose?

They were both sitting there, hands on their knees, looking at me. My head went back and forth. I felt sick to my stomach. I didn't want to hurt either one of them. At that point in my life, this was the hardest decision I had ever had to make. I was so conflicted. *Oh my God, I love them both. Who do I pick?*

In the end, I picked Granny, which was the right choice, because she was Mom's mom. But I remember feeling so bad for Nanny that when Granny went into the room to meet Brett, I went out and sat on Nanny's lap because I didn't want her to feel left out.

—

I miss Nanny and Granny. I miss the time I spent with them.

Those women set a powerful example. To be reared among hardy, stalwart Southern ladies is a mixed blessing. I am the better for it, but I am also slightly cowed by their independence.

Contrary to what some folks might believe, Southern women are not needy. Nanny and Granny showed me firsthand that Southern women can achieve anything they desire on their own. If men are in the picture, it is because the women allow them to be there.

Let's just say that if I ever get above my raisin', I'll have no shortage of hands ready to yank me back down.

I will never forget where I come from. My family wouldn't let me.

—

When I was a kid, I thought that it would be nice if Nanny and Granny could move in together. I fantasized that they could share a big house and garden and look after each other as the years passed.

Now that Brett and I have moved out, Nanny and Granny don't see each other as often. But when they do, they're both proud, doting grandmothers.

Granny generously shares that title. And Nanny is happy to take it.

For eight months Clayton and I lived between two houses. I left my first husband with just Clay's diaper bag and the shirts on our backs.

I remember when Clayton was about two I told him to stop doing something because he may fall and get a black eye, and he said, "Like you had, Mommy?"

—Faye Parker

CHAPTER FOUR

Be Aware That Not Everyone Will Like How You Sound

My *birth father*, Vernon Grissom, had gray hair by age twenty. It was curly and lay heavy on his forehead.

He sported a paunch. He'd lost a handful of his teeth by age twenty-three, thanks to a heavy chewing tobacco habit. He was also a drinker and a smoker. Somehow he still managed to be handsome. He had a charming smile and enough self-assurance to seduce everyone he came across, especially women, whom he found difficult to resist.

I remember he looked much older than he was—especially next to my mother, who has always radiated warmth and youth.

Vernon wore giant, out-of-date glasses, with big, square tops that covered half of his face. They were tinted. When he had them on, he reminded me of George Jones.

My memories of Vernon are few and fragmented. The most vivid image I have of my birth father is of him sitting in his easy chair in his living room. It was a long, narrow room, with couches on two sides and a television at the end. Every time I'd visit, I'd lie on one couch, while Grandma Grissom, his mom, would sit on the other couch and crochet and he would sit in that La-Z-Boy recliner and play solitaire on a big piece of plywood. He rarely said anything. He just sat in the chair and played solitaire.

I would be lying if I didn't admit that when I sing this song, I think about him.

> *Another day*
> *A lonely day*
> *So much to say that goes unspoken.*
> *And through the night*
> *His sleepless nights*
> *His eyes are closed*
> *His heart is broken.*

> —

Everybody has a different way of coping with calamity. Some people become reclusive. Some people confront their problems in an emotional way. Some people become the victim. And some people just laugh about them.

I'm a laugher.

I think that happened because my mom is the type of person who doesn't let things bother her. She'll laugh about things that most people wouldn't.

When it comes to getting through life, laughing at it sure beats crying.

There were times when I was angry with my mother letting herself fall prey to men who were unkind to her. Men who would tell her to shut up whenever she disagreed. Men who barked out rules and always had to have the last word.

My mother is an independent woman. She's principled and strong. But I think she's got—and she'll be the first to admit it—a penchant for abuse. She's attracted to men who like to exert power. Stubborn, strong, bossy men. And I really don't know why.

When I would worry about her, she'd always say, "I know when to leave." She let me know her relationships were her choice.

I think that because of the type of men she chose, I opted to be different. I saw one way of interacting with women, and I decided to try something gentler.

—

I believe my birth father was an exceedingly lonely man. The only thing I ever saw him do was shuffle cards for solitaire and sleep. I know he was in a band before I was born. He was an incredible musician. He could pick up any instrument and play it just by ear. He was never formally trained, but he knew his stuff. Music was in his blood.

Vernon had dreams of singing professionally, but they never came to pass. He drank too much. Although many country musicians have managed to drink and sing, my birth father wasn't one of them. The bottle consumed the rest of his life. He worked for NAPA Auto Parts for a while, and later, at a filling station. He quit that job to take a position at the garbage dump. All day he would sit there by himself, watching people drop off their junk.

He married twice. My mom was his second wife, and after that, he didn't marry again, which was probably for the best.

I remember going to downtown Wake Forest with him, to a house right across from the Southeastern Baptist Theological Seminary. He introduced me to some woman, and then I hung out downstairs while the two of them disappeared for "a visit." Twenty years later I know what they were doing, but at the time I was just a scared kid sitting alone in an unknown house, wondering where his daddy had gone.

From age three on, my birth father would pick me up from my mom's house every other Saturday.

We'd drive down Highway 98 and go directly to the video rental store to pick up four or five videos, enough for me for the weekend.

We'd go to his house, I'd pop 'em in, and he'd sit and play solitaire till he fell asleep in his chair. I remember that he snored really loudly. I'd try my best to politely cough or make a loud noise so he'd wake up. I didn't really want to wake him up, but I did want him to stop snoring.

In between videos, I'd cook my own frozen dinners. And that was the weekend.

—

I know my birth father was a drunk. But I don't remember ever seeing him intoxicated.

I must have been only four years old when he drove me home under the influence. I didn't know it until he pulled up to drop me off, and my mom instantly became upset.

She yelled at Granny to take me into the backyard. And then she got Dad—my stepfather—to come around to Vernon's car. Dad was very ticked off. He was red in the face and shouting. He threatened to pummel Vernon. I don't know if he actually did, because my Granny yanked me behind the carport.

Aunt Mary Helen told me that Vernon sobered up by the time I was eight. If he did drink, I never saw him do it. But he still smoked like a steam engine.

—

After I got a little older, I still visited my birth father every two weeks.

I would phone him and ask him to pick me up. I don't know why I did it. I guess it was just something to do. I'd call him and sometimes I'd go to his house and I'd watch a movie just like I did when I was a child.

Soon enough it became two months between visits. Then three months. And toward the end of school, I'd wait eight and nine months before I picked up the phone.

No matter how long I waited, he never called me. He always excused himself by saying, "I don't like talking to answering machines."

I said, "Well, hang up if you don't want to talk on the answering machine. You don't have to leave a message if you don't get me at home. Or if you do, just say, 'It's me, call me.' "

He didn't.

This went on until I turned sixteen.

About that time I finally got my driver's license. I called my birth father and I told him that I didn't need him to come pick me up anymore, but that I would still love to spend time with him. I told him to call me when he wanted me to come over to the house. I figured we'd visit every few weeks.

He never called again.

———

So I moved on.

The last time I saw him it had been more than nine months since our previous visit. I took him a video of a show in which I sang with a band.

He said, "That was pretty good, but the band wasn't following very well."

He'd been in a band, and he knew something about how bands should work. My band wasn't up to snuff. He didn't say anything about my singing. It was as if he hadn't heard me at all.

———

After I turned seventeen, I started singing in a variety show with a local band. We performed every other month. My birth father's family would come and hear me. It was a good clip for them to drive from Franklin County to Johnston County, but they made the trip. They wanted to be supportive. Vernon never came.

I think at that time I started asking myself, *What is the point of having his last name?* It was a stubborn, rebellious thing for me to do but it made perfectly good sense. I didn't want to pass his last name on to any children I might have when it meant nothing to me. I asked myself, *What would I tell my kids when they asked where they got their name from?*

I entered a stage when I decided, *You know what? I should be ashamed of some of this.* So I asked my mother what she would think if I changed my last name to her maiden name. She made me speak with my grandparents to confirm that it was okay with them. They said yes, so we did the paperwork and that was that. I was no longer a Grissom. I was an Aiken.

This displeased a few people on my birth father's side of the family. But I didn't care. I wasn't trying to forsake anyone. I was trying to find myself.

—

Even after we ceased talking, Vernon sent me a birthday card every year. For many years, it was the only contact we had.

The cards were always intended for children. It would be my seventeenth birthday and he'd send a card with a picture of a talking bunny or a puppy on it.

Inside, they just said "Daddy." That's all. "Daddy."

I remember I would open those cards and I would want to be so angry. I would want to laugh about them, to ridicule how stupid they were. I longed to pretend they didn't matter to me. But in some small way, they did.

They meant he still cared. That somewhere inside he knew he had a son. And he remembered the day his son was born.

My birth father died on February 2, 2004.

I was scheduled to sing in Raleigh the day of the funeral. When I found out about his passing, I was saddened, but I didn't cry. I decided I should keep my commitment to the show and opted not to attend the service. I chose not to mourn, but to sing.

—

Could things have been better with my birth father? Absolutely. Do I wish things had been better? Probably. Do I think my life would be better had things gone differently? Probably not.

You can't force people to feel things they aren't willing to feel. Not everyone will love you the way you want them to. I learned this lesson early, but everyone learns it eventually.

I never asked Vernon for anything. I tried to be what he wanted. I strove to make him proud. But he was deaf to me.

Still, I survived. And I kept singing. And in time, other people listened.

That's what I tell people who have missed out on having a parent. Take your act somewhere else. As my mom always said, "People are lonely because they build walls instead of bridges."

My birth father showed me what happens once you shut down your heart. Still, I sing about him.

There was a man, a lonely man
Who lost his love through his indifference
A heart that cared, that went unshared
Until it died in his silence.

I think about him.

And Solitaire's the only game in town
And every road that takes him, takes him down
And by himself, it's easy to pretend
He'll never love again.

And always, I feel sorry for him.

Another day
A lonely day
So much to say that goes unspoken.
And through the night
His sleepless nights
His eyes are closed
His heart is broken.

Use disappointment as material for patience.

—Faye Parker

CHAPTER FIVE

Find Your Voice

When I *was young,* I was teased by other kids like it was their job.

I recall riding the school bus and always sitting in the seat right behind the bus driver. I would talk his ear off and hope that the kids behind me wouldn't tease me and that if they did I wouldn't hear it.

I wasn't very popular in grade school. I had friends, but they were kids like me—geeky, shy, unable to fit in. I was a different sort of kid. Some of it came—and I hope my mom won't get upset by this—because I spent a large chunk of my childhood around nobody but adults.

My mother and I left my birth father when I was

two. After that, I spent most of my time with her or my grandparents. I would even go to work with Mom at Sears and hang out with all the ladies there. They'd prop me on the carpet samples and make me sing them country songs. With my red hair, square white teeth, and freckles, I looked like Howdy Doody, which for some reason they found adorable.

I felt comfortable when I was singing for the ladies at Sears—or singing for anyone, for that matter. But kids in grade school don't really care whether you can sing, and since I'd rarely spent any time around other people my age, I didn't know the social rules.

I knew how to talk to adults. I knew all the words to "Break It to Me Gently." But neither of those things keeps you from getting wedgies at recess.

It didn't help that I dressed like a loser. I wore Bill Cosby sweaters, the ones with the loud patterns and crazy colors. At school, I'd look around the classroom and all the other kids were wearing HyperColor neon T-shirts, Umbro athletic shorts, and designer sneakers, and I was wearing an old-man sweater with a collar and tan pants.

Mom bought my clothes. I don't even think I had a say. And if I did have a say, I would ask for some name brand that we couldn't afford. So basically, I wore a lot of nerdy stuff.

I remember that I wanted new tennis shoes, and my mother said, "We don't have the money for hundred-dollar tennis shoes. Besides, you don't grow from having everything given to you." And then she'd tell me about Dolly Parton and where she started, and she'd say, "Look where she is!"

Well, I didn't want to be Dolly Parton. I wanted to be cool.

My wardrobe would have been forgiven if I had been athletic. But I was clumsy, spastic. So there I would be on the playground, dressed like somebody's grandfather, burning up in those sweaters, unable to play soccer or kickball—just me off by myself, looking and feeling ridiculous. So of course I was picked on. I was teased. I was dodgeball bait. I spent a lot of time praying to be invisible.

Middle school was the worst. Middle school is where everybody goes through that change, trying to figure out who they are. Kids feel threatened at that age.

Feeling threatened, I became somewhat reclusive. It made me a little bit quieter, and I tried to stay out of everybody's way. When the bullies felt threatened, it meant that they were going to go on the offensive, and who better to go after than the quiet kid in the corner?

There was this game called Wall Ball that the kids liked to play. The slowest kid would end up standing against the playground wall and the other kids would pelt him with a ball. One guess who that might have been.

My best friend was a boy named Chinh. Kids who

are picked on flock together. People always find their support group. My mom used to say, "The water finds its own level." So you have the picked-ons, and the pickers. Chinh and I were picked-ons.

Chinh was Vietnamese, so he didn't speak much English. People picked on him, but he really couldn't understand them, so they gave up after a while. Chinh and I became good friends. I always ate lunch with him because he was nice and he didn't tease me—not even when my mom wrote inspirational notes on the outside of my lunch bag, which was practically every day.

The friendship between Chinh and me also probably had something to do with the fact that from a young age, I always kind of gravitated toward the people who were outcasts. I understood them. I knew how it felt inside to be judged and made fun of, to feel different and to pay for those differences.

As a child, I had another friend, a black girl who wore giant glasses and a hearing aid. We used to hold hands when we walked down a busy street. Safety in numbers.

Once, one of my aunts saw us together and rushed home to call my granny. "You won't believe what I just saw," she prattled, implying that what I was doing was somehow wrong.

Granny just laughed.

—

Usually I walked home from school with Natalie, who was also the child of a single mom. She never had anywhere to go after school. Natalie was lonely and a little scared. Once I figured that out, I started bringing her back to my house. We would play, and my mom would cook her dinner. She just seemed so happy to have a place to be where she wasn't alone. I was happy, too. It was refreshing to spend time with another kid who wasn't trying to knock my glasses off, a kid who spoke English.

Back at school, my survival tactic was to be nice to everybody. My mom taught me—wrongly, I learned—to just be kind to the bullies and then they'd come around. But when you are a geeky, gawky kid with orange hair, glasses, and old-man sweaters, they don't come around. Little boys don't one day wake up and say, "Gee, my yanking that little boy's underpants out of his corduroys is mean-spirited and I should really cut it out."

Those boys learned pretty quickly that I wasn't going to fight back and I wasn't going to tattle on them. The nicer I was, the bigger the target on my forehead. The high road left me defenseless. And the mockery only got worse.

"Retard."

"Fag."

"Wimp."

"Dork."

"Four eyes."

"Loser."

I got it all. But the thing is, the more I took it, the less I cared. Being harassed became a part of my day, and I accepted it.

I know it sounds sad now, looking back, but at the time I wasn't analyzing it. I was just living my life. I think the bullying helped me figure out at an early age that stuff is going to happen to you that you wish wouldn't. People are going to treat you badly, and ultimately that is out of your control.

"Just let it roll off," my mom would say. And I did. Because even as a kid, I knew the other option wasn't for me. I was not going to hurt somebody else.

—

Now, my mom didn't make it any easier for me.

I was a born talker. Even though I was the odd kid out, I chatted in class. I think I believed that if I was cute enough I would win everyone over just like I did the ladies at Sears. The teachers proved harder to impress.

My mom warned me that if I was reprimanded for talking in class again she was going to come to school in her curlers and sit with me all day long.

I said, "Yeah, right, like Vicki Lawrence in *Mama's Family*?"

And she said, "Exactly."

I didn't believe her, so I kept on cutting up. Lo and behold I show up at class one day and there is my mama already sitting in the classroom.

Now, thank you Jesus, she didn't do the curlers; she came dressed, and she sat beside me all day long in every class.

Every class. All day.

And I'll tell you what, for a little boy who's getting picked on already, to have his mama come and sit beside him in class all day long, it ain't too helpful.

I can still see her in the English classroom, sitting right in front of me—just sitting there, her back straight and her head cocked, while the teacher talked. All the other kids were snickering and nudging each other. They stared at me like I was some new breed of loser. I sank into my seat and ground my heels into the floor.

I remember praying, "Lord, please let me fall right through this floor now and die." Because being the school nerd was one thing, but being a nerd whose mama comes with him to school was an unprecedented low.

I knew that the next morning the kids would subject me to a fresh arsenal of abuse. At the time, death really did seem like a better option.

—

And then I entered seventh grade.

Leesville was a brand-new school, just built. It was a long building made of brown brick. Since the school had just been opened, no cliques had been formed yet. Everyone was starting fresh. I got an idea that maybe things could be different there.

In spite of what my mom wanted, I hadn't joined the choir in sixth grade. I thought it was too lame. I had sung in elementary school but had given it up, trying to be like the other boys, none of whom sang.

I had also had a bad experience with the Raleigh Boychoir, a prestigious singing club made up of boys who lived in the greater Raleigh area. These were boys who lived in bungalows instead of houses, boys who would ultimately go to boarding school, boys who rode horses and played lacrosse, boys whose parents listened to NPR.

My mom listened to country station WQDR, and we lived in a raised ranch house north of town, down the street from a Wendy's. I knew my voice was just as good as those of the other boys, but I never felt at home in the choir. I was intimidated. I hated singing opera. The Raleigh Boychoir became just another place to get picked on. So after a year, I quit—which annoyed my mama.

She always said to me, "God gave everybody a calling, and He gave you a voice. He gave you a talent, and you need to use the talent He gave you."

Instead, I made the tragic mistake of deciding to be the water boy for the football team. I figured if I could be part of the team somehow, I might be respected. I figured wrong. The boys on the team mocked my high voice, and Coach Leary called me a gnat.

Because I was ignoring her about singing, Mom took it upon herself to approach the new school's music teacher, Mrs. Norton, and let her know that I needed to be in her choir.

Mrs. Norton called me into her office after school. She said she had heard about my previous choir experience and asked if I would be interested in trying out. I said I wasn't sure.

She explained to me that she believed music brings people together, that it is a universal language. She also mentioned that a lot of cute girls would be taking the class. Then she popped in a cassette and asked me to sing.

I sang Whitney Houston's "One Moment in Time." (I was still a soprano then.)

Mrs. Norton was enthusiastic. She told me I had a strong voice, that I could project a long way.

"You sing in church, don't you?" she asked.

I nodded.

"I can tell. You sing like you're aiming for the rafters."

She flattered me, telling me that voices as strong and steady as mine don't come along that often.

"You are already connecting the words to feelings," she said. "I know adults who can't do that. You've already joined passion with ability." She seemed genuinely impressed.

Then she reminded me about the girls who would be in the class.

"We'll be rehearsing before school," she said.

So I thought, *You know what, I'll do it. And if it's stupid, so what? I'm going to do the singing thing anyway.*

And I did it, and things got a little bit better.

To start, I had an automatic group of friends, a show choir clique. And the more I sang, the more people knew who I was. It stopped being about the glasses and the bad clothes. It became about what I could do.

In grade school everybody else had something they excelled at, and I didn't have anything. That's probably part of the reason I was so vulnerable to teasing. I wasn't known for anything. I was just that kid—that dweeb—who wore the Cosby sweaters and had his mom come to class.

Choir led to other things. I decided to work on the yearbook. I was the copy editor, and I did everything no one else wanted to do. I worked really hard and did a good job. And I made more friends.

By eighth grade, everything had changed. I had a really wonderful year. I usually got the solos in the school shows. Sometimes I even got standing ovations. Everybody knew me, not as the gangly redhead but as the kid with the big voice. Well, they knew me as both. But my looks were no longer a liability. It was like they were thinking, *He may be geeky but that boy can sing, you know?*

—

I am still close to Mrs. Norton. We see each other occasionally. And when I see her, she always reminds me of the power of music, of her belief that singing allows all of us to feel passion, to be connected in a fundamental way, that there is a reason every culture makes music, that there is a need in this world for song.

Though she no longer teaches at Leesville, she still flatters me. "You have a one-in-a-million voice, kiddo," she says. "You are working that range."

I often think that if Mrs. Norton hadn't pushed me, if she hadn't kept after me, I may never have joined choir and singing might have fallen completely out of my life.

I remember this every time I sing: how it is essential to hear your calling, and how it sometimes takes a person you barely know to help you find your own voice.

To make it through life, you need faith to cling to. And laughter. I've seen Clay laugh off the pain sometimes. I tell him it's okay to show people your real feelings. I guess you teach your kids to be strong in the places where you're weak.

—Faye Parker

CHAPTER SIX

Learn More Than One Song

My birth father taught me by his example all the things I never wanted to be.

He did sing. And by all accounts, he had a nice voice. He and my mother used to perform together. She wore sparkly pantsuits, he buttoned on a snazzy shirt, and they covered country tunes by Roy Acuff and Tanya Tucker. Music may be what brought them together, but singing isn't enough. Not when you drink. Not when you resort to violence to make your point.

My mother married Ray Parker, the man I call Dad, when I was seven. He was a big, barrel-chested guy. He had a jolly face, usually embellished with a mustache. He looked young for his age, partly because he dyed his hair dark to hide the gray. Dad never walked; he strutted wherever he went. He was very proud of himself, good or bad.

After he left the Air Force, he worked at a prison. He also worked at Sears for twenty-five years, which is where he met my mother and courted her with his confidence and a box of candy. I remember he would always wear his Sears pin. It had a ruby in it, which indicated twenty-five years of service. He'd put it on the lapel of his suits, which were inevitably hideous. For some reason Dad could never wear a plain navy or black suit. He favored aqua or pink or peach or plaid.

He gravitated toward the tacky. He once had this T-shirt made as a gift for my mother that had his face printed on the front. When he gave it to her, she just laughed. There was no way my mother was going to wear a shirt with her husband's face on it. So *he* wore it.

We have one photograph in the house that captured him best. It is a portrait taken of him in his correctional officer's uniform. He's standing in front of the American flag. If you look at everybody else's picture, they are stone-faced and tough, but in his, he is laughing.

—

Dad was a good man, but I don't think he ever knew what to do with me. He was, as my mother said, a man who could love only his blood kin. And I wasn't genetically his. I was, literally, the red-headed stepchild.

This meant that our relationship was strained. He had inherited a kid who didn't have any of the same interests as he did. I liked music; he liked shooting deer. I think we felt in competition for Mom's attention.

Once Brett was born in 1985, the situation became more pronounced. Dad wanted to have Brett. I think he wanted him so that he could have a connection to Mom, something that only he and Mom had, something that I didn't have a part in. I'm glad Dad loved Brett, but the contrast between Brett and me only made matters worse.

Brett was enamored of Dad, and Dad of him. Dad had his boy. From my perspective, my role in the family had been filled by someone else. And the dynamic between Dad and me grew prickly.

In my mind it seemed as if Dad really relished punishing me. He would spank me until I was bruised, then blame me for bruising so easily.

When I was twelve, he sat me down to talk. He said, "When other parents tell me they love their stepchildren as much as their real children, I don't believe them. It's just not that easy."

I don't think he knew how to love me.

I don't think he ever considered me his son.

—

In many ways, Dad was a very good person, an honest person. He was family oriented. He liked to have fun. Everybody who knew him liked him. But I think it was very difficult for him to love some kid he met when the kid was seven.

He tried. Now and then he would take me to Four Oaks, where he was raised. We would visit with the rest of his family, and they were all extremely welcoming to me. Then he and I would go to this tiny used car lot he owned, and he'd have me clean up the vehicles. After we worked for a few hours, we'd go to Thornton's Restaurant.

Time stands still in Four Oaks, and Thornton's was no exception. It was a soda shop where they made trademark hamburgers that they grilled flat like a cheese sandwich. I thought they were the best thing I'd ever eaten, so I ordered one every time.

Dad knew everyone in Thornton's. It was a simple, friendly place, and he always seemed so much happier there. Even so, I could tell he still felt awkward around me.

Kids that young know when they're wanted. They are very intuitive. And I'm sure I was the same way. It felt to me as if he wished I weren't in the picture.

When I started getting older I didn't really have any desire to try to make our relationship better. I had given up by that time. I felt I might have made a mistake even calling him Dad. I had come to wish that I had just called him Ray from the beginning and let him earn the title of Dad. I began to feel in my heart that I was never meant to have a father.

There was Vernon, the every-other-weekend guy. And there was Ray.

———

When I was young—eight or nine, right after Brett was born—Mom asked whether I wanted Dad to adopt me. I said no because I didn't know what it meant. I didn't know whether it meant that I was never going to see my birth father again.

Now I wonder whether it would have made a difference. If he had adopted me and I had been Clayton Parker, would that have made a difference? Would that, in his mind, have triggered something that said, *Okay, I can love this kid now*?

By the time I was in high school, things had gotten so bad that I would hope to God Dad wasn't around when I came home, because he always sent me to my room. He didn't seem to want to see me. This was painful because he loved Brett so much. They were close. Dad made it very clear to Brett that he wanted him around. And Brett could get away with anything he wanted to. I, on the other hand, could not.

Mom would beg and plead to get Brett to clean

his room. He wouldn't do it. I would clean mine. Then Dad would mess it up so that I had to clean it again.

One day he said my room stank like dirty shoes because I never cleaned it up. And it *was* rank in there. But I knew that the stench wasn't mine. So I looked around, and, lo and behold, he had hidden stink bombs under my bed.

I never knew why he did things like that—as if he wanted to make my life more difficult. He would mow the yard in squiggly lines and then make me mow after him and mow it right. He would take things off my bookshelf, throw toys on the floor, and then tell me I was messy. He would make me clean my plate but allow his other children to eat what they liked.

One day he bought a new car for my stepsister, Amy, his daughter from his first marriage. She had just graduated from college. The car was a convertible.

Dad said, "The whole family is going to take a ride in Amy's car."

I was very excited to go. But then he said no, I couldn't go. I had to clean out the freezer. So they all drove away and left me there. It felt as if he was taking a moment to create his ideal family.

—

After I left for college, Dad got sick. His illness shifted things inside me.

I grew up a little, and I realized that, deep down, Dad wanted to be a good father to me. He never knew how. But he did the best he could.

His illness gave him a softer heart. And it softened mine, too, to see him compromised like that.

I remember the first time he was unable to walk up the stairs. I had to come up beside him and take his arm. He couldn't breathe. He just looked at me with pain in his eyes.

His sickness had made him vulnerable, and he had never been vulnerable. Dad always had the upper hand. He would tell Mom that he was the king of the castle, even though she earned the money. That's kind of how he ran the house. He was the master of the domain.

When he was sick, the posturing fell away. Dad became approachable. I wanted to have a relationship with him, only I didn't know how.

—

As he lay dying in the hospital, I struggled. His sickness was far harder for me than I expected. I guess I always secretly wanted him to be my father.

I wanted somebody I could call Dad and mean it. Someone who was proud to call me Son.

His frailty seemed to be a window for me, a

chance to make amends. I thought, "That way I can say this is my dad. This is my father."

But I never made amends. I was afraid he would reject me. I kept thinking there would be more time. One more day.

And then he died.

—

He had been ill for seven months. My relationship with him was more fulfilling in those seven months than it had been in the entire time we lived together.

I learned more about him in that time, and more about myself. He was a human being just like I was. He had his bluster and I had my theatrics, but fundamentally we weren't that different. Both of us could be obstinate. Both of us thought we knew best. At the end, I was finally able to see him less through a veil of anger than with empathy and heart.

In the last eight weeks of his life, Dad couldn't move. He couldn't walk. The tissue in his lungs had hardened, and he would cough a lot, choking up at dinner, his eyes wide with unbearable panic.

By February 2002, he had to be placed on oxygen support.

By April, he had to be on it twenty-four hours a day.

By the first week in June, we had to put a bed downstairs for him.

A week later, we took him to the hospital, to the

emergency room. He'd had a horrible attack. But he insisted on coming home. He wanted everybody there on his last Father's Day. He knew that he was dying.

The next day, he went into the hospital. He would never come out.

For four days, he was asleep all the time. At that point I decided that although he might not be able to talk to me, I was going to talk to him. I began crafting my speech. All those things we never said to each other—I was going to say them.

But I didn't.

I never brought myself to get everybody out of the room and do it. There was always that barrier.

—

In the end, I'm grateful to him for Brett. And I'm grateful to him for making my mother happy, because he obviously did. He made her happy enough that she wanted to marry him and spend the rest of her life with him. They had good times. I'm very indebted to him for that.

When I look back on him, if I really sit down and am introspective, I cry. I know he tried his best with me.

I miss what I think could've happened, the relationship we could've had. And I hate that, for whatever reason—his fault, my fault, nobody's fault—we didn't have that.

—

We were all in the hospital when he died at nine o'clock in the morning on July 4, 2002.

I had been up all night and had just fallen asleep. When I woke up, I heard the nurse say, "It's over."

I still wonder whether, had I had one more chance to say goodbye, I might have done it. But I didn't. And now I completely regret it. I screwed up.

My cowardice kept me from expressing what was in my heart.

—

I planned the funeral. I think I wanted to do it for him. When we knew he was dying, I wrote his obituary. In fact, before Mom got home from the hospital I had already checked out funeral homes and picked a good one. I had everything ready.

I wanted to be close to him. And when I look back on it now, I am thankful that I knew him when he was vulnerable.

I value those memories of the time he was sick, when he was a little more selfless and I was a little less haughty. Odd as it may sound, that's kind of the way I like to remember him.

That last Father's Day, all of Dad's loved ones were at the house. He took each family member— Mom, Brett, Jeff, Amy—into his room to talk, one by one. They all came out, one after another, crying. He was saying goodbye. Dad never called me into the room. He never got around to saying goodbye to me.

I think he was scared, too.

—

My mom told me a story recently.

A friend of my dad's was visiting the house and he said, "A few months before Ray died we were riding around in my car, just driving. He was talking about Brett, how he knew he'd join the military and grow into a fine man.

"Then he looked out the window and said, 'And my other son is going to be a famous singer one day. He has the most beautiful voice.'"

The Lord sometimes takes us into troubled water not to drown us, but to cleanse us.

CHAPTER SEVEN

Sing from the Heart

My brother, *Brett,* is seven years and nineteen days younger than I am.

When I was six, my mom and dad took me on a vacation to the Great Smoky Mountains to tell me that Brett was coming. They made it an event. I think my mom was worried that I was going to be upset or jealous. She wasn't sure how I would handle a new baby demanding her attention. But I was thrilled. I told her I wanted a baby sister. I had this notion that I would be the big protector.

As it turns out, Brett did not need any protecting. He was a hearty boy. He was popular. He was everything I had never been.

I kept waiting for the day when Brett would come home from school crying and I would march over to some kid's house and teach him a lesson. It never happened. Brett didn't need me.

We loved each other. But we were raised very differently.

I was raised by my mother and Granny and Nanny. Brett was more of Dad's kid. He grew up wanting to hunt and play in the woods with guns. Everything Dad loved, Brett loved. Dogs. Sports cars. Watching old westerns. *The Big Valley* television show. Brett wanted to be Dad.

As a toddler, Brett couldn't say "Clayton," so he called me Dodo. It was his nickname for me. My dad loved that. I was Dodo long after it stopped being cute.

—

As Brett got older, he began to realize that the rules at home were different for him than they were for me. He noticed how Dad treated me. It put him in a terrible position.

He loved Dad, and he loved me. I think he would have been happy if we could have all gotten along, maybe gone hunting together. I think he had this fantasy of us being tight, the way the brothers and father are on *Bonanza*—robust and respectful, with a lot of meaningful backslaps being passed around.

Once, after Dad had sent me to clean my room

for the third time, Brett said to him, "You're not being fair." Dad ignored him. Brett often tried to run interference for me. I returned the favor by trying to talk Mom out of punishing him. I think I had a greater success rate.

Brett and I respected each other, but we didn't have a great rapport. Because he had friends, we didn't relate. Our life experiences were so dissimilar. After I left for college, we became more useful to each other—mostly because I knew that, unlike me, he occasionally drank alcohol. And I knew he wanted to keep it from Mom.

I always told Brett I would drive from Charlotte and pick him up if he ever was drunk enough to require a ride home. He never was, but he did party. And Mom did find out. It was then that I had to explain to her that I was not a normal child.

Going to parties and having a beer in a plastic cup and sneaking a cigarette in the school bathroom and skipping the occasional class to go see an Adam Sandler movie—that was what typical male teenagers did. They did not join the show choir and abstain from swearing and call their mothers even when they were out on a Saturday night date.

Brett was a normal teenager. I explained this to Mom and told her she should be satisfied, because, although Brett might be drinking now and then, he was a heck of a lot happier than I had ever been in school. I also told her she should stop living in denial. I advised her to be more understanding of Brett.

Brett appreciated that, and we became closer. Then Dad died, and everything was amplified.

—

As soon as the nurse told me Dad had passed away, I bolted from my chair and ran to find Brett.

He was in the waiting room of the hospital, pacing. I rushed up and hugged him. I was crying. He knew immediately what that meant. He sank to the floor.

He had just turned sixteen.

—

I wanted to be the one who told Brett. I don't know exactly why. I just wanted it to be me; I wanted to be there for him. I had this feeling that for the first time in his life, he might really need his big brother.

I remember thinking, *He's only sixteen. He has so many milestones to come. And now he'll have to face them without his father.*

I wanted to protect him. I had always wanted to protect him. I suspect I always will.

Watching Brett hurting in the days before Dad died, I understood for the first time what it meant to have a dad.

People were consoling me, but I thought Brett should have been the focus of that attention. However, Brett is stoic. I remember when Dad was ill we had some family over and Brett went out and sat in the driveway. I went with him. We just sat there side by side. We didn't say anything. We didn't need to.

—

Right before Dad died he bought a brand-new pewter-colored Firebird. He knew he was dying, so the Firebird was really for Brett. He didn't say that, but we all knew.

Brett loved that car. He and Dad would spend hours tinkering with it, popping open the hood, cleaning the dash with Armor All.

Dad was able to drive the car only four times before he got too sick. That car was how Dad showed Brett how much he loved him. He told Mom he wanted to leave something for Brett to remember him by. Mom wasn't so crazy about Brett driving around in a sports car, but she knew how much that Firebird meant to Brett, so it stayed.

The problem was, after Dad died, we couldn't afford the car. The payment was too high, as was insuring it for a teenage boy. Mom told Brett we had to sell it, which was tough.

Brett understood. He gave the Firebird up really graciously. But it was another piece of Dad that had slipped away.

—

In 2003, I had just come off my first year of making any real money. I knew I was going home to Raleigh for Christmas, and I had an idea.

First, I paid off Mom's house. She had mortgaged herself to the hilt and was only scraping by. I kept it a secret and put the payoff statement in a giant garment box to present it to her.

Then I bought Brett a navy blue Firebird. I hated that it wasn't pewter, but I had looked as long as I could and time had run out.

I kept the car hidden in the neighbor's garage. Come Christmas Eve, I asked Brett to open his gift. I knew I couldn't sleep if he didn't.

I'd given him a little gift bag with the keys dropped inside. I put a stack of video games on top. He opened the bag and saw the videos.

"These aren't the right kind for my machine," he said. "I have an Xbox, not a PlayStation."

"You can exchange them," I said. "I put the receipt in the bottom. Dig it out."

Brett fished around in there and found the keys. He knows cars so well that he didn't have to be told it was a Firebird.

He grabbed the keys and held them in front of his face. All he could say was, "No way." He said it about twenty times. "No way. No way. No way."

I said, "Let's go wake up the neighbors."

It was around 11:30 at night, but we knocked on the door and got them to open the garage. When

Brett saw the car, he jumped into the seat and started the engine—but not before he hugged me.

—

When people ask me which was the happiest day of my life, I always think back to that Christmas Eve. Being able to get back something for Brett that had meant so much to him. Being able to pay off Mom's mortgage. Nothing has ever felt better than that.

Brett is serving in the Marines now. I write him a letter every day. At the bottom, I tell him to be careful, be safe. I still have the urge to protect him. I sign the letters, "Love, C.A."

Just the other day I was riding on the tour bus, watching the trees tick by, and I found myself thinking about Brett—about the boy he used to be, rowdy and fun. And about the man he is now, serious and wanting to serve others.

I realized that even though Brett is easily one of the most important people in my life, I have never told him that. We didn't develop that sort of relationship, the kind where we say things out loud. For some reason I've rarely been able to say "I love you" straight to his face. I can tell my mom every time we speak. I can even tell many of my friends. But not Brett.

It occurred to me that in that way I am exactly the same as my dad. He always said that men talking about feelings was "too mushy." Perhaps that's what kept me from saying goodbye to him.

There is nothing worse than regret. Once experienced, it is uncorrectable. But it is avoidable.

Brett is away now. For how long, we don't know. And I would never forgive myself for being a coward about something as important as my affection for him. So the next letter I write, I'm telling him the truth: That I need him. That he matters.

It may be mushy, but I'm okay with that.

Abuse can go either way. You can decide you're going to be the same as the person who hurt you, or you can decide you're better than that, and that you're going to survive. And I'm just glad Clayton picked the better side. You can drown in pity but he knew that wasn't the way he wanted to go. He was determined not to let anything break him.

—Faye Parker

CHAPTER EIGHT

Don't Be Afraid to
Sing Out Loud

Before I entered high school, I killed time playing with three neighborhood friends I'll call Jonathan, Dennis, and Benjamin.

Both Jonathan and Dennis were jocks. Benjamin was more of a skinny outcast like me. Ben had relatives in the military, and we would go over to his house and play army.

Ben, Dennis, and Jonathan took turns pretending to be the general. I was always a private. They would make me run in place and do push-ups, which was kind of a joke, seeing as I could barely do any. As a kid, when I got nervous, my left eye would dry out, and it would drift to the side. Ben would see it and yell, "How dare you look away when I'm talking to you, Private!"

I kept waiting for my day to be an officer, but it never happened. Soon enough, playing army got a little old. So we decided to start shoplifting from the drugstore down the block.

The three of them stole sunglasses, cologne samples, candy, and magazines. They dropped all of it down their baggy track pants as they sidled down the aisle.

Every day we would go to the crawl space under Jonathan's apartment building and lay out the loot. Jonathan and Ben kept trying to outdo each other—a contest that culminated when Jonathan stole a skateboard, which his parents unfortunately discovered and promptly confiscated.

I remember itching to impress Jonathan and Ben by stealing, but then, when it was my turn to shoplift, I could never do it. I'd joke and say I didn't have the track pants. But the real reason was that I was worried about what my mom would say if I got caught.

Being afraid of your mama pretty much condemns you to permanent lameness as far as preteen boys are concerned.

———

Once high school started I tried to compensate by acting out in class. I did this primarily in choir.

Our new teacher, Ms. Lawrence, wasn't very popular. She took music seriously, and most of the students in the class did not. There was an idea that voice class was meant to be easy, like driver's ed or shop. Ms. Lawrence hoped that we would all learn to read music and absorb classical terminology, theory, and history. Everybody disliked Ms. Lawrence, so for me the choice was simple.

One of the first things she did as our music teacher was to give us a test on musical terms. I took the test, but I made up jokes for all the responses. A "bar" became a place to get a drink, a "key" unlocked a door, a "note" was something you pass in class. Ms. Lawrence was not amused. She failed me.

And then she called my mother.

The two of them went to the principal and worked out a solution for my insolence. I spent the next afternoon cleaning the boys' bathroom with a toothbrush. My mom said it wasn't because I failed the test, but because I had chosen to show so much disrespect.

I had wanted to prove to the class that I hated Ms. Lawrence as much as they did. But I didn't see any of them in the bathroom scrubbing toilets.

—

A few weeks later, my mom took me to see Ms. Lawrence perform in *Oliver* at the Raleigh Little

Theatre. She played Nancy. When she sang "Oom-Pah-Pah," her voice was so strong, the hair on my neck stood up. I remember sitting in the crowd and almost being jealous. I wanted to be up there.

After the show we went backstage. It was a pivotal moment for me. Every person I saw was doing something I enjoyed. And there were so many people! The whole idea of working on a show was mesmerizing.

I realized that Ms. Lawrence was a woman who deserved to be paid attention to. So I did. I retired my class clown act—which never really made me popular the way it always seems to in the movies—and I began to concentrate on singing.

This was easy because, although I had made some improvements, my geek factor had not exactly vanished by age fourteen. I was still riding the bus, which in high school in Raleigh is not cool. And my mom had made me get a job.

"Who works at fourteen years old?" I whined.

"You do," she said.

—

I got a job bagging groceries at Winn-Dixie.

It was there that I met Brian Hutchinson, who happened to be one of the cool kids at school. He was on the soccer team. He was a big outdoor guy. He was incredibly popular. And he was never ashamed of me. This set him apart from the other cool boys, who used to either ignore me or point and whisper when I walked by them in the hall.

Brian was an independent thinker, which in high school is saying something. He wasn't put off by what I seemed to lack.

The better I got to know him, the more I realized that he and I weren't that different. We both had things we excelled at, sports for him, singing for me. He wasn't smarter than me or funnier. What set him apart was that Brian did his own thing and didn't care what people thought about him. He was confident, so others flocked to him.

And that's when I decided, *I'm going to stop worrying about everybody else.*

—

It took years, but I determined, finally, that it would probably be easier to be the person I was meant to be than to rework my personality in order to make an impact on someone else. It wasn't a complicated notion. But before Brian, it hadn't occurred to me.

I focused again on singing, on the thing I knew made me feel happy inside and brought joy to others. I performed in shows and at assemblies. I still made the choice not to drink or do drugs. I worked a little harder on my studies, although I confess that my grades stayed average. I went to church. I bagged groceries.

I did the things I liked to do. Once I made the choice to finally be myself, all of those guys, the popular guys, started acting friendly toward me. In time, we began to hang out. When they would get drunk at keg parties, I would drive them home. Now and then, they even came and watched me sing.

These are guys who played sports and chugged beer and didn't have any interest in musical theater. But they came to my shows. Not because I was so great, but because I was finally self-assured.

Not only did they come to watch the shows, but after I sang, you could hear them whooping and hollering in the rafters.

—

By senior year, I was just as popular as anybody else. I joined the student council. I was in charge of homecoming. I headed up Winterfest. I did the announcements on the intercom. I had gone from being the school bottom-feeder to being one of the most well-liked students in school. It was surreal.

My recognition had nothing to do with anything external. My mama still wouldn't buy me nice clothes. I still had big old glasses and hair that nothing could be done with, mainly because my mom cut it in the kitchen with a towel wrapped around my neck. I was still skinny and uncoordinated.

The only thing different about me was how I felt about myself.

—

Last I heard, Brian is married and living in Wilmington, North Carolina. He works for one of the corporate offices of Young Life, a Christian youth group. He is, by all accounts, relaxed and content. Just as he was in school.

Brian never knew what he did for me. But he changed my life. He changed my life because he dared to live his.

It's ironic to me how women go berserk over Clay now.
They never even noticed him before.

—Nick Leisey, childhood friend and right-hand man

CHAPTER NINE

Consider Singing a Duet

In high school, there were three girls who improved my life beyond measure.

The first girl was my friend Jessye. Jessye was an outcast like me. She was chubby and I was skinny, and together we made quite a picture. Maybe it was because we had nothing to lose that I was willing to steal a car to go and pick her up one Saturday afternoon.

It wasn't stealing so much as jumping the gun. The car was actually going to be mine. My dad owned a used car lot, and he brought home a 1989 Ford Escort for me. It was bright red, with a hatchback. The gearshift was on the floor, not on the steering column, which to me was very fancy. It also had the sort of seat belts that slide across your chest when you sit down. In short, it was in my eyes the coolest car I could ever hope to drive.

But I had to wait until I was sixteen. Until then the Escort sat in the yard.

A few houses down from us lived Carrie Clouse. Carrie had been driving from the time she was eight years old. Not just sitting on her daddy's lap, either. She had her own set of keys. She had been chauffeuring her friends around since she was thirteen.

I wasn't the best driver, but I figured if Carrie Clouse could do it so could I. I had received my permit when I was fifteen, which meant that I had passed a written exam at the DMV qualifying me to learn to drive with an adult in the car. The fact that I hadn't actually done that yet deterred me little. The first weekend day both my parents were gone, I decided that Jessye should come over for a visit.

I called her and announced that I was coming. Then I waltzed out to the car, hopped in, and turned the radio up as loud as it would go. The song was "I'm Free" by Jon Secada. I will never forget that feeling of climbing behind the wheel and hearing "I'm Free" blaring from the speakers.

Once Jessye and I got back to my house, we realized we were hungry. There was a Little Caesars pizza place down the road, but I wasn't about to walk now. We piled back into the Escort and headed off to the restaurant.

I parked the car in front of Little Caesars and went inside to pick up the food. It was at this precise time that my dad drove by and spotted the Escort. I glanced out the window and all I saw was him, storming up the sidewalk.

I bolted from the Little Caesars. But it was too late. I was praying, *Lord, please don't let him unleash his wrath inside, in front of all these nice people waiting to get their "pizza pizza."* We met right at the door. He reached for my belt loop, snatched at my waist, and started spanking me.

He spanked me with such ferocity that an old man who had also been waiting for his pizza came out and told him to stop.

"Interfere again and I'll hit you, too," my dad shot back.

He dragged me home in his car, leaving Jessye behind with the Escort—and the pizza.

Back at the house, my mother was waiting. When she heard the story she made me write five hundred times, "I will not ever drive without permission again."

It turned out to be a waste of time. They sold the car.

—

My mom got almost all of her life proverbs from old country singers. Elvis. Brenda Lee. Dolly Parton. She loved herself some Barbara Mandrell.

When I would suffer for being a doofus, she would say, "Just look at Barbara Mandrell. She was country when country wasn't cool."

Audra Brown also loved Barbara Mandrell. Audra was my best friend from childhood until college. We met in church as kids and quickly became inseparable.

Looking back now, I realize that I had a serious crush. But as a kid, she was just this girl who smelled nice and whom I saw every day.

Audra was the most willful person I ever knew. And she was just as stubborn as me. We would fight, fight, fight.

When we were in high school, our nights out would go something like this:

Me: It's so sad about working mothers.

Audra: Well they should be home if they hate working so much.

Me: But they can't stay home and feed their kids.

Audra: Then they should have thought of that before they got pregnant.

Me: That is ridiculous.

Audra: You're ridiculous!

Me: Oh my God!

Audra: Oh *my* God!

Angry silence.

Heavy silence.

Then, after a few minutes . . .

Me: You wanna see a movie?

—

Once during dinner at the Olive Garden we got into an argument because Audra snapped for the waiter.

I said, "You don't snap at someone."

And she said, "It's his job."

Our bickering escalated into a full-on fight. I don't know whether it was hormonal tension or what, but it seemed we were always at each other's throats. We'd scream at each other. She would take the preposterous stands. But I loved her too much to walk away.

I liked Audra because she was strong, independent, and the epitome of the Southern Belle. She knew how to work a man. She used her womanly wiles to do it. Audra had studied Scarlett O'Hara, and it showed.

At the same time, she was fiercely independent.

When you met Audra, you knew what you were getting. She was never ashamed. The stuff about my life that made me uncomfortable—not having enough money for name-brand sneakers, not being cool—she celebrated. We were both country, but she was the only one of us who didn't wish it were different.

There was something about Audra that made me feel at ease. I was a progressive mama's boy. She was a conservative daddy's girl. But we loved each other. I was myself around her. I didn't ever feel the need to pretend to be someone I wasn't.

———

I ended up taking Audra to her senior prom. She always had to have a boy on her arm, and I filled in when she didn't have a boyfriend, which wasn't often. Normally, she dated Marines.

I wore a tuxedo, and she wore a ball gown. Before the prom, we climbed up on her trampoline and jumped in our formal wear while her mother took pictures.

I'd like to say we didn't squabble that night, but I think we did. I do know it wasn't the worst argument we ever had, because when that happened, I was driving on the highway and I kicked Audra out of the car and left her on the side of the road.

As I pulled away, I peeked in the rearview mirror and saw that she had removed her top. I slammed the car into reverse and yelled, "Put on that shirt right now and get your butt back in this vehicle."

And she said, "How else was I supposed to get a ride?"

She was afraid of nothing.

———

It was Audra who came with me to my grand-mother's funeral.

Grandma Grissom was my birth father's mother, the woman who helped take care of me whenever I visited Vernon. I was home for Christmas break, and Mom woke me up one morning and said, "Your Grandma Grissom died last night. If you want to go to the funeral I'm happy to go with you."

I knew Vernon might be there and I also knew I wasn't going to be exactly welcome, but I wanted to pay my respects. So I said, "Thanks, but I want to do this by myself."

Then I called Audra.

———

I remember the funeral home was very quiet and there was a long corridor outside a large parlor area. As soon as we entered the hall, I spotted Vernon hanging around the main room. I jumped a little and stood in the corner, too nervous to continue down the hall. I hadn't seen him in more than five years.

One of my cousins, Sarah, saw me hiding out, then walked over to whisper something to an attendant. Not a minute after, the funeral director came into the hallway and found me lurking in the corner. He shook my hand, then said, "I'm going to have to ask you to leave. The family doesn't want you here."

—

As we were leaving, I handed Audra the keys to the car. I was distraught. I didn't want to drive.

Audra climbed behind the wheel and began wrestling with the seat. Then she messed around with the steering column. She grunted and sighed until finally she threw the keys in my lap.

"I can't figure this car out. You're going to have to drive us out of here. Or you can just sit there and sulk. Your choice."

I glared at her. But I got up and took the wheel.

As I was driving, it dawned on me what Audra was doing. She didn't want me to waste my tears on people she deemed unworthy. She didn't have patience for people who were afraid of looking life in the face. She was strong. So she forced me to be stronger. She dragged me out of self-pity.

"So what now?" she said, looking at me as I drove toward home. "You want to see a movie?"

I did. I wanted to be anywhere Audra was.

—

Erin Cates was the most desirable girl in my high school. She was sweet and beautiful. She had dirty-blond hair and full cheeks that flushed when she smiled, which was often. And she had a terrific voice, which I got to hear every day in choir class.

Because we both did shows, we were invited to attend the masquerade ball held by the Raleigh Little Theatre. When Erin heard about the ball, an amazing thing happened. She asked me to go with her.

In my mind, this was going to be the biggest night of my life. I was going to wear a tuxedo. I was going to buy her a corsage.

My mom knew how badly I wanted to go. I had been going on about it all week. But then, two days before the dance, I talked back to her. I sassed my mama, so what did she take away? My one chance with the homecoming queen.

—

By this time I was working a job at the Italian Oven, washing dishes. I worked most nights in the back, where no one would see me. Erin knew where the Italian Oven was. I mulled it over, and I decided that some opportunities simply cannot be ignored.

The night of the ball, I told my mom I had to work. I dressed in my Italian Oven uniform— a button-down shirt with logo patches and black cords from Structure, which just happened to be the coolest pants I owned.

I hid my tuxedo (which was unfortunately a tad too small) in the trunk of the car, said goodbye to my parents, and left for work.

Erin met me in the Italian Oven parking lot. She picked me up and drove me to the Kroger grocery store, where I changed into my tuxedo in the men's room. She wore a pale aquamarine gown, and when I saw her waiting for me there in the fluorescent light of Kroger's, I knew she was the most beautiful girl I'd ever seen and that any punishment would be worth this night with her.

The dance itself was mildly disappointing. It was filled with old people. I was hoping for lots of kids from our school—witnesses, who would see me on a date with Erin Cates.

Nonetheless, Erin and I danced together. We *slow danced* together. The song was a ballad by Boyz II Men, and I remember how dizzy I felt, spinning in circles, my hand on the small of her back.

I remember thinking: *We have so much in common, both of us love singing. And she's from a good family and she seems to be enjoying herself and maybe, after tonight, she will say she wants to be my girlfriend. We will become a couple, and we will always remember this dance as our special night.*

I dreamed that dream the whole time we danced, and then the ball ended.

We drove back to Kroger's. I took off my too-tight tux and put on my Italian Oven uniform, and Erin Cates, homecoming queen, waved goodbye and drove out of my life. I didn't even try to kiss her good night. Because although I longed for something different, I knew the truth: Erin Cates was never going to be my girlfriend.

Erin Cates liked me as a friend. She appreciated my voice, and the fact that I was a gentleman. And that's why she spent time with me.

Still, I know she cared about me. Because even though we both knew we were destined to be just friends, for one night she let me pretend otherwise.

—

These girls—women now—showed me how life should be lived.

Take risks.

Stand up for what you believe in.

Imagine what can be.

Mostly they reinforced a notion I had already gathered from my own mother: Women make good company.

And if you're going to steal a car, go to a funeral, or attend a formal dance, it is a woman you want to do it with.

Clayton was never shy. He might pretend he was shy so people would beg him to sing. I saw him do that quite a bit. But he was the type of child who would sing for a stranger. He was never afraid of opening his mouth. He was just brimming with song.

—Granny Aiken

CHAPTER TEN

Some Songs Are Sung in a Minor Key

In the fall of 2000, I left Raleigh for college in Charlotte. The summer before I left, I got a call from my half sister, Deb, my birth father's daughter from his first marriage.

Deb was twenty-two years older than I was, so she was really more of an aunt to me. I viewed her as an adult, and I remember when I was a boy visiting my birth father, Deb would often come over and rescue me. She would take me to her house, and I would play with her sons, who were about my age. It was the most fun I ever had when I went to Vernon's place.

After I changed my name to Aiken, Deb was one

of the only members of the Grissom family who seemed to understand. She kept in touch with me even after my birth father stopped bothering. Now and again she'd send a letter or call to chat. I saw her every Christmas. We'd visit at her house and catch up. I was closer to her than to any other Grissom family member.

Right before I left for Charlotte to go to college, Deb suggested that the two of us go out to dinner. She left me a message that she had some things she wanted to talk with me about.

For some reason, I got really, really scared. There was something in her tone that put me off. I assumed she wanted to talk about Vernon or my changing my name. We had never really discussed those topics. I was about to head off to my new life, so I decided I would take a pass. I didn't want to revisit dark times when I was on the brink of something so new. I wasn't prepared to dig up a bunch of emotional stuff. I was thinking about the future.

So I never returned her call. I put it aside until I forgot about it. Then I left for Charlotte.

—

During February of my first year of school, I was in my apartment getting dressed to go to work when the phone rang. It was my mother. She told me to sit down. Then she said that Deb had shot herself. She was dead.

I fell behind the couch onto the floor.

I had never felt so unhinged. I remember thinking, *This is what shock feels like.* Time stood still. A horrible, frozen moment.

Then I began to wail. I screamed. My mother was on the other end of the phone, crying, trying to console me. But I was unreachable. I yelled so loud that the neighbors came to the door.

"My sister is dead," I cried. Then, in my head, *It's my fault.*

"My sister is dead."

I never called her back.

"My sister is dead."

What have I done?

—

I know in the future there will be things that affect me as much, but to date nothing in my life has disturbed me as deeply as my half sister's suicide. To me, it came out of nowhere. I didn't see it coming. I didn't get a chance to say goodbye.

From the moment I heard the news until today, I have wondered what I could have done to prevent her death. If I had returned her call, if I had met her for dinner, would she be alive today? Was she reaching out? Was she hoping to say her farewells?

That night in the apartment, I cried for two hours straight—just screamed and screamed and screamed.

Then I packed for Raleigh.

—

There was to be a wake and a funeral service. I planned to attend both. My mother said she would go with me.

If anything illustrates the type of woman my mother is, it's the fact that she had the guts to go to Deb's funeral. Mom knew she would be surrounded by people who had shunned her. She had every reason to believe my birth father would be there—a man who had beaten her, a man she had fled. But she wanted to help me.

So, uncomfortable or not, she went. She brought along Nanny, who also had reason to be ill at ease. But I thought I owed it to Deb, so the three of us donned our mourning clothes and drove to the funeral home.

When we arrived at the wake, there was a line out the door. I was crying when we pulled into the parking lot, and I didn't stop sobbing the entire time. I remember how crappy it felt to have to stand in line, with people looking at me bawling, wondering who I was and why I was so upset. Most people were unaware of who I was. I wanted to be in the family receiving line. I felt like I was still her brother, even if other people in the Grissom family disagreed.

As we waited, I thought about all those days I had spent as a boy playing in Deb's backyard with

Me and my birth father, Vernon Grissom. I was eighteen months old. This is one of the few pictures I have of us together.

The mandatory Southern shot of the baby in the washtub. This was taken at my Granny Aiken's farm.

Granny and Papa Aiken sitting on Mom's couch in a rare moment of rest.

Easter Sunday. I was sitting on our swing in the backyard impatiently awaiting my chance to eat some Easter candy.

*My uncle had a band in Johnston County, and
sometimes my mom would sing with him for fun.
This time, I was invited up.
It was one of my earliest performances.*

Check out the teeth! I was around seven and playing in my yard at home in Raleigh.

On one of a couple trips to White Lake in North Carolina. Brett loved the lake. I was a little bit afraid of the water. Note that my hair is doing the Opie thing that will plague me the rest of my life.

Dad's birthday. I think Brett is trying to tell me that my glasses are too big for my face.

Mom took this in the back of one of Dad's old cars.
He collected vintage automobiles and kept them at a lot
out in the country.

Halloween. Brett was an urchin, Mom was a clown, and I was Robin Hood. Only ten and I'm already mugging for the camera.

Brett and I were chorus members in the Christmas show at the Raleigh Little Theatre. The show was Cinderella and I played about seven small parts. I was fourteen years old.

This was taken during a family trip to Arkansas. Dad liked to take us on boat tours. I was sixteen years old and terrified of drowning, so I can only imagine I was not having the greatest time.

Handsome Brett at sixteen, the year Dad passed away.

Signing autographs backstage at the Charleston, South Carolina, concert in 2004.

More autographs. My tour manager, Mary Brennan, is standing beside me, helping to keep the line moving.

A photo op backstage in Lexington, Kentucky. My fans love to tell me funny stories. I think they see me as a friend rather than a celebrity.

In the tour bus, waving good night after the show. Fans will sometimes wait for hours just to say good-bye.

Working in the tour office backstage, reviewing the merchandise list, an hour before curtain.

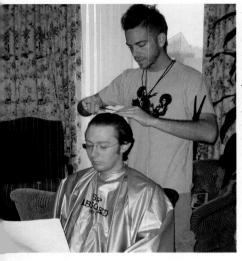

My stylist, John, is cutting my hair in my hotel room in Baltimore. When we tour, there is no time to go out, not even for a trim. What you don't see in the picture is my dog Raleigh trying to eat the clipped hair off the carpet.

My right-hand man, Nick, and me on the bus, on the way to the next show. Behind me is the television we watch The West Wing *on every night during dinner.*

Me scared out of my mind driving the tour bus through North Carolina. Our driver, Sarge, had to take a bathroom break, so I volunteered to sit behind the wheel for him. Never again. That bus was huge!

Signing my poster backstage at the meet and greet.

Happy days in Roanoke, Virginia.

Working the line. After a show, I often walk to the security gates and shake hands with the fans who have been gracious enough to wait. A lot of times they scream for my dog Raleigh more than for me. She definitely has her own fan club.

Outside the venue in Syracuse, New York.

Filming with Quddus for "Backstage Pass" on MTV's TRL.

Danny, Angela, Derek, and Al—four members of the band, getting ready to walk onstage.

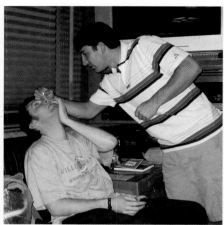

Okay, I know this looks pretty lazy. The truth is I had a sty and I couldn't get my medicine in the right place. Thank goodness Nick had no hesitation about squirting burning fluid into my eyeball.

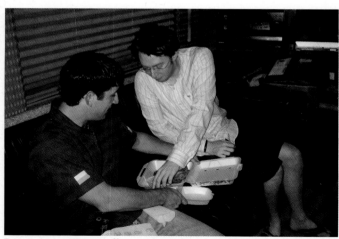

Dinnertime. We usually eat around 11:00 at night, after the show is over and we have wound down a bit. My favorite meal on tour is chopped steak, with peach ice cream for dessert. I probably eat a half gallon of Breyers peach ice cream a day.

Looking out the bus window in Baltimore, Maryland. It took us a while to exit the parking lot that night. One woman even chased the bus on foot!

Another city, another meet and greet.

Raleigh trying to escape and hit the open road. Sarge feeds her pretzels, so keeping her in the back is a real challenge.

Nick is carrying a goody bag given to me by a fan. Jerome is laughing because I'm telling them how a woman in her sixties just goosed me as I walked by!

Bus fun. Nick, me, Mary, and John trying not to kill one another after riding together on the bus for two months and ten hours.

*The finale of the show.
I'm singing "Solitaire."
Derek Wyatt is my drummer.
He is so shy, he said that
if he could play from
backstage he would.*

This is the part of the show where we ask someone from the audience to dance with us. I do this so that I don't have to dance, because people do not want to pay hard-earned money to see that.

S'Von Ringo, Quiana Parler, and Jacob Luttrell, doing what they do best. If Quiana or Jacob had been on American Idol, *I would not be where I am today. Their voices are incredible.*

Me, my co-author, Allison Glock, and her daughters, Dixie and Tilly, hanging out preshow in Knoxville, Tennessee. Tilly seems particularly riveted by me.

My beautiful mother, Faye Parker.

her children, Jeffrey and Casey, while Deb watched us from the kitchen window. I remembered her grinning—how happy she seemed back then, looking after us, a passel of kids running wild and free in the sunshine.

After an hour, the line finally moved and we made it to the room where the family was receiving visitors. I saw that Aunt Mary Helen was there, but my birth father was not.

I had half expected him not to come. Deb was the only friend left in my birth father's life, his only remaining connection to something like love. I predicted that the inescapable finality of the wake would have been too much for him to bear. Deb was still so young. She would have been forty-five years old.

—

When the line rounded the corner, Aunt Mary Helen saw us and walked over to my mother, Nanny, and me. She gave my mother a hug. Then she gave Nanny a hug. Then she began to walk away.

I turned and fell on her. I threw myself at her chest, bawling. I felt out of control. I was this big, wet mess, trying to crawl into an old woman's arms.

I wanted absolution.

I wanted her to know I hurt.

She pushed me back. She waited until I could stand, watched me a minute, then left.

—

The next person in the receiving line was George, Deb's husband. He was trembling, but he reached out for me. He understood that Deb and I had a father in common, and no name change or circumstance would alter that.

"She wanted to talk to you," he said. "She really wanted you to be a bigger part of her life."

I cried more and squeezed his shoulder.

"Talk to her now," he said. "Please, just talk to her now."

Nanny went to the coffin with me. It was an open casket. I remember grabbing Nanny's hand. And I remember feeling her pull me off of the casket because I couldn't bring myself to leave. I wanted to stay there, as if I could still make a difference, as if it weren't too late. I wanted Deb to know how sorry I was.

—

All three of us likewise attended the funeral the next day. I felt marked because by then most people knew I was the very estranged son of Vernon. There were a lot of eyes on me.

We sat down in our pew. We had arrived early. As more mourners filed in, the ushers wanted us to scoot over to make room. I didn't want to move. I remember feeling welded to the seat.

Nanny told the deacon, "He's family and he wants to sit on the end."

I remember how strange that sounded to me. Like an ax against a metal ball.

Family.

—

After it was all over, I walked toward Aunt Mary Helen. She had drifted away to the family car. I don't know why, but I marched all the way across the cemetery, right up to her, and grabbed her.

"I'm sorry," I said, beginning to cry yet again. And I was sorry.

That I hadn't tried harder.

That I had failed Deb.

That Deb was gone.

That our lives weren't different.

That we weren't able to live together as a family.

That love wasn't enough.

I was sorry about all of it.

"You know," Mary Helen said, "she was so proud of you. You hurt her so badly." Then she stopped talking and ran away from me.

There was nothing left for me to do but go back to the car. I remember sitting there, surrounded by all the other vehicles, not wanting to move, not wanting anybody to speak. I didn't want my mom to talk; I didn't want Nanny to talk. I was stunned. I wanted silence, something to quiet the howl in my head, something heavy and black to disappear into.

I decided I should go see my birth father. I thought that maybe he needed me. And at that moment, I wanted nothing more than to be of some use.

We drove past his house. I slowed down the car. I tried to look inside the windows, but the shades were drawn.

I took it as a sign and drove on.

—

Since then, I have had only limited contact with Aunt Mary Helen.

I've had to learn that when families break apart, there will be casualties. Some bridges cannot be rebuilt. Tragedies happen. And blame gets passed around.

Deb's death shook me to the core. I see now that you cannot take loved ones for granted, that the people you count on may not always be around.

I understand also that the people you care about don't always behave in the ways you expect they will—for better or worse.

—

When my stepfather died, my mom and I got a card and flowers from Aunt Mary Helen. Reading the card, I considered for the first time how she must have felt when my mom fled with me, when her own brother was arrested and was someone to be feared.

I thought that maybe in her mind, she had tried to make up for my birth father, to fill in for what she saw he wasn't doing. She knew the truth.

And then I remembered something I hadn't thought of since I was a boy. Aunt Mary Helen was an organ player at her church. When I was young, she would take me from my birth father's house to her home, and the two of us would sit at her piano and play.

We sang old hymns, and she let me bang on the keyboard. She never got angry when I made a ruckus. She just kept on singing over the din.

—

I got a letter from my aunt not too long ago. It said, "We're watching you. We're proud of you."

It wasn't a long letter. But it said enough.

To put Christian principles into practice through programs that build healthy spirit, mind and body for all.

—The YMCA doctrine

CHAPTER ELEVEN

Learn to Read Music

I *started working* at the YMCA when I was seventeen years old because I needed a job. I began with a program called Y Life, which took place every Thursday night. The counselors would visit the Raleigh housing projects, pick up some kids, and bring them back to the Y for dinner, games, and exercise.

After I graduated from high school, I stayed on with the Y. I had not committed to college yet. I wasn't sure what I wanted to study, and in truth, I wasn't ready to leave Raleigh. I was taking a handful of random classes at night. But my days were free, and restaurant work had gotten old. So the Y became my full-time job.

I was ill prepared for how this one decision would alter the course of my life.

—

Initially, I enjoyed the work because, for once in my world, I got to be in charge. I could tell these kids what to do. As an added bonus, I looked real good to the people around me.

Honestly, the whole gig was about feeding my ego. I didn't necessarily see that I was making a difference, but everybody else assumed I was, so it was a nice badge of honor to wear. *I work with underprivileged children. Pat me on the back and give me a cookie.*

While I was there, I made some friends and acted up like teenagers will—like the time I rolled this other counselor's house.

She and I did not get along. We argued, and in my mind, she was not kind enough to the kids in the program. So in a moment of puerile behavior, I drove to her house in the dark and threw toilet paper all over the trees in her front yard.

The next day she told me what happened. I asked if she knew who had done it. She said she didn't know exactly, but that she was sure it had to be a girl because the toilet paper was only hung on the lowest branches.

That was a proud moment.

—

The next summer I went back to the YMCA to work full-time at the summer camp. I was still really relishing feeling my influence over the kids and the praise I was getting from other people who saw my job as a sacrifice. But I had also started to enjoy myself more. Almost imperceptibly, the kids began to get to me.

And that whole thing about having people think I was doing this wonderfully good deed stopped when I actually began to feel the difference I was making.

I felt it first with a little boy I'll call Joey.

—

Joey was a handful. When we were assigned our list of kids, our "huddles" at the beginning of the session, everyone dreaded getting Joey. He was a troublemaker.

I got him the summer after his third-grade year. When I did, all of the other counselors said, "Oooooohhh."

Joey had a mean streak. He tended toward violence. He wanted to be the loudest person in the room, the center of attention, and whoever took the focus away from him paid for it. Joey never really cared for anybody else; making friends didn't matter. He came from an environment that had taught him if you want it, you better take it. And if you have it, you keep it.

Basically, Joey was too smart for his predicament. If you live in a housing project, people tend to have low expectations of what you can do. Joey was hobbled by those perceptions. He had intelligence but no resources with which to exercise it. Hence, he turned to mischief.

I remember one time I was walking with him outside of camp and he stumbled, falling on the pavement. It wasn't a major catastrophe, but when he got up he had his hand on his head. He was crying, and he said his vision was blurred. I asked him to move his palm away from his forehead, and when he did I saw blood.

I went into emergency mode. I said, "We need to get you to the office immediately, clean you up." Inside, I was panicking.

Joey began to giggle. It turned out that the blood was a handful of berries. He had been planning his ruse for twenty minutes, and he had done all of this to amuse himself.

I was ticked off that he had scared me. But I was also impressed. He was nine years old—and faking a concussion is not your typical nine-year-old trick.

—

I began to understand that, like me, Joey was a little bit of an outcast. Most of the kids from his housing project played football or basketball. Joey never did. He was interested in electronics.

I liked the challenge of Joey. I felt an unlikely kinship with him. I knew what it was to feel like you didn't fit in.

There was another little boy I'll call Ethan, a chubby kid with the friendliest spirit you ever saw. He was always trailing after Joey, and Joey used him whenever he could. He made Ethan carry his bags and buy him candy. Ethan didn't mind. He just wanted to be liked.

As the weeks progressed, Joey and I continued to connect really well. I started to let him get in trouble just a little bit, and then when he needed it, I would push back slowly. We got into a rhythm of working together. The greater our progress, the less I wanted to blab about it to my friends.

I went from using my job as a way to impress others to wanting to keep it to myself because it felt so personal and good. It became my private thing. Like a spiritual journey, I didn't want to cheapen it by turning it into an anecdote.

The summer wore on, and Joey continued to make unexpected progress. We became close. He felt safe with me. We trusted each other. He was still Joey, but he was more controlled and he was responsive.

On the last day of the session, the YMCA gave an honor to the most improved camper. The other counselors and I discussed it and we decided that the best camper was Joey. We felt he really deserved the recognition. He'd never been rewarded before; he'd always been punished. So at the final assembly, we announced, "The reward for most improved camper goes to Joey!"

Joey was shocked. He didn't know what to do. I walked over and handed him the prize, a little electronic basketball game that he got to take home with him. He was so thrilled you'd have thought we'd given him tickets to the NBA play-offs. He couldn't stop grinning. He held the game close to his chest and hugged it hard.

It was the final assembly, so the Y director said, "Does anybody want to stand up and say what they're thankful for?"

Of course, all the counselors stood up and said they were thankful for the kids who were in their huddle and for such a great summer and how terrific the campers were. Then some kids stood up and said they were thankful for their counselors and for the director and the YMCA.

And then Joey stood up.

—

We were all fully prepared for Joey to say something impish to make everybody laugh, to try one last time to get some attention.

But instead he stood up and he said, "I'm thankful for my counselors, Clayton and Tisha, and I'm thankful for the YMCA, and I'm very thankful for my best friend, Ethan, who I treat bad sometimes but is still my best friend."

Then he walked over to where Ethan was sitting and handed his new basketball game to him.

The whole assembly was weeping. It was a great moment, not just for Joey, but for me as well—seeing him make a positive change in his life and choose generosity over covetousness.

No one told him he wasn't being nice to Ethan; he figured it out himself. He knew it. And then he did something to make amends.

He had changed. He had overcome.

—

After Joey, I was hooked. Helping kids was going to be my future. I didn't know exactly how yet, but I felt in my gut that I could never return to my previous life of egocentric pursuits.

There are so many kids in this world who could use another person looking out for them. Someone who will help them to discover their strengths and rise above their weaknesses. Someone who offers another opinion of their worth.

Why not me?

I know you cannot win every battle. Not every

child can be saved. But this does not give you an excuse not to try. If you quit, all is lost. In the end, you can't give up on people, because you never know what marvel lies underneath.

Joey showed me that.

Clayton was always able to relate to all the children. They wanted to be around him because of his energy. And because he really tried to touch each child's life. He would work extra hours. He'd pick out songs to sing especially for them. One thing I thought was strange was that when he sang he never wanted people to look at him. I think he was embarrassed.

—Kristy Hall, longtime friend and project director for the Bubel/Aiken Foundation

CHAPTER TWELVE

Even the Best Singer's Voice Cracks

I *continued to work* at the YMCA the next year. Every session brought a whole new batch of children, and with them, new lessons.

One morning, a camper I had never met got off the bus and ran straight over to give me a big hug. I was surprised, but I embraced her back and said, "Welcome to camp."

A few weeks later I went up to her and said, "Tracy, remember that first day, you came right off the bus and gave me a hug. You didn't even know who I was. Why did you do that?"

And she said, "Well, you were wearing the YMCA T-shirt, so I knew you'd be my friend."

At that point I realized it would be a challenge to find another job that could make me feel that good inside.

I feel that even now. Singing in front of a stadium of fans is wonderful, but it pales in comparison to being embraced by a child.

—

After a few summers I was recruited to join the largest branch of the YMCA in Raleigh. The man who brought me there was Jeff Flake.

Jeff was the YMCA director, and unlike other men I knew, he didn't have to be right all the time.

Initially, I didn't want to leave my local branch. I liked working with the at-risk kids, but this new job paired me with a far more well-heeled demographic.

Jeff told me that he had seen me speak with passion at YMCA fund-raisers and that it was his intention to hire only counselors with that kind of energy for the job. He wanted to make that particular camp the best in the state, and he felt that with the right type of staff, he could.

Jeff quickly became my mentor. He made sure that every kid felt confident, every parent felt comfortable, and everybody he hired was responsible. He took a lot of pride in his programs, and he instilled pride in a lot of us. He loved his senior staff. Jeff was an observer, a real listener. I never saw him lose his temper ever. Not once. He was one of those people who command attention without being belligerent or bossy. He had a refreshing way of leading: He hired people he had faith in and allowed them to do their jobs.

He had a particular interest in me. He took care to show me how to fit in with all types of people, how to manage big personalities (skills that have since proved handy), how to best effect growth in the kids. He was grooming me for a future at the Y.

I admired Jeff's steady, graceful leadership. He was an authority figure with heart, and that inspired me. He became one of the only people outside of my family I wanted to make proud.

—

In time, the YMCA became a second home to me. I loved what it stood for. It was a place where everybody was accepted, no matter who they were. It was a kind of utopian society. Regardless of what was going on in the outside world, at the YMCA everyone was a part of the team.

Jeff trusted me to run a camp of 150 kids. I had twenty teenagers who worked on my staff. Some of them were the stars of the soccer team, some of them the head cheerleaders, and some of them the computer club members. We had all the demographics covered.

What I concentrated on with them was team

building. Jeff was all about team building and being what he dubbed a "servant leader." The week we were hired, Jeff made us all wash each other's feet. He wanted us to know how it felt to serve and to find honor and purpose in that service.

Because of Jeff, I wanted each person who worked with me to treat everyone else with respect. They may not have been kind to one another at school, but while they were at the Y, they behaved like friends.

The other counselors nicknamed me Gonzo because I was weird and I just did my thing. I wasn't afraid to make a fool out of myself. I might dress up as a gorilla—anything in order to do my job well.

I didn't mind if the other teenagers who worked for me occasionally laughed at me. What I cared about was what Jeff valued: serving the kids.

I believed that if the other counselors thought themselves too cool to play the game or be ridiculous in the skit, then they were missing out. Kids don't need lessons in cool. They need to have fun.

—

Throughout the season, my respect for Jeff continued to grow. In truth, I probably admired him a bit too much. I began to view him as perfect, as the model of the man I wanted to become. Whenever I had questions about life, I asked myself, "What would Jeff do in this situation?"

Soon enough, a situation presented itself. I met a little girl I'll call Rene, who had a developmental disability.

Until Rene came along, the YMCA had not admitted special-needs children. The higher-ups claimed there wasn't enough staff. But once I met Rene, I felt I couldn't turn her down.

I told the YMCA administrators, "I will take her around with me all day if I have to, but we're not telling her mother that we can't take her. We can't do it."

I begged Jeff to allow Rene into camp, and ultimately he agreed. It was difficult, but I thought we made it work. Rene thrived at the Y.

—

Because of Jeff—or more precisely, because of my wish to impress Jeff—I began to take my job at the Y very seriously.

Jeff made sure that everybody had a role. His style of leadership was so unlike anything I had previously experienced. He knew that people don't listen to you if you start handing down orders. People don't respond to being bossed around. They like to be a part of whatever's going on. If I learned anything from him it is the value of making people happy in their jobs. That if they have a stake in their position, if they have ownership over what they're doing, then they want to make it work.

I became so invested that I developed my own ideas about how the camps should run. For example, I instructed my counselors not to pick a favorite camper. I'd explain that when Sally's mom drops her off at camp that morning she doesn't give a flying fig about any other child there because the most important kid at that camp to her is Sally. And she better be the most important kid for you, too, whenever you're around her. And then when Teddy gets there, he better be the most important kid. Because children know when you have a favorite.

I went to that same camp as a boy and I can tell you I wasn't the favorite. I wasn't as athletic as some of the other kids who played soccer. I was freckly and didn't like to get near the pool because I burned. Basically, I wasn't as much fun for the counselors, and I knew that I wasn't the favorite kid, and knowing that stunk. I didn't want any other child I worked with ever feeling like I did.

— ⊞ —

At the next session, the YMCA brass told Rene's mother that her daughter could not come back. They weren't willing to restructure my position so I could work with her. I was beside myself.

Even worse, I learned that a Down syndrome

child had been refused admission to one of the YMCA programs. After a dispute with the parents, the Y had offered the child a spot but required that the parents provide a private caretaker for the kid, which was ridiculous. Because why would anyone pay both a private caretaker and the Y? To me it seemed like just another way that society excludes special-needs children. This did not sit well with me. I believe the YMCA stands for inclusion. The YMCA's mission is to put Christian principles into practice through programs that build healthy spirit, mind, and body for *all*. It doesn't say "for those who are high-functioning." I turned to Jeff for advice about changing the long-term philosophy of the YMCA, but it seemed to me his mind was elsewhere.

When I tried to press Jeff, I felt that he was turning away from me. It seemed almost as if his will to serve had run dry. He clearly had other things on his mind; selfless service no longer seemed to be the first and most important thing on his agenda.

I was devastated. I learned that Jeff wasn't flawless after all. He was human.

—

Jeff's fallibility wounded me for many reasons: Because I needed him. Because I wanted to be him. But mostly because I admired him so much.

In many ways I was like a child who believed in the unimpeachable righteousness of one man, turning him into the idealized father I'd always wanted, without considering the person he actually was. No man could have withstood my scrutiny or naive expectations.

Today, I worry about falling from grace. I know that good men do not stay good if they become consumed by ego. I know how easily you can stumble off the path if you look in the mirror instead of looking ahead.

I don't want all the good work I plan to do to be eclipsed by selfishness. I want to stay connected to the right, real things: helping children, building camps, training teachers to continue to aid the cause long after I'm gone.

I am in a position where for the first time in my life I could be a dictator if I wanted to. I am the boss. I could turn into a real brat. But because of the lessons Jeff taught me, I stay between the lines. I'd rather build a team. I want the people I work with to feel good.

Jeff ran the best YMCA camp in the state. Everyone flourished under his tutelage. He taught me what it means to be a servant leader—to gain from giving.

In the end, his frailties were a blessing to me.

Knowing that every man, even the best man, loses his footing every now and then has allowed me to forgive my own slips. No one is perfect. Because of Jeff, I have learned the value of forgiving not only others, but myself.

The first time I met Clay he seemed like such a genuinely nice person. He popped his head into the makeup room and made some silly noise. I thought he looked like a cartoon character. I've known him a year now, and he's a goof. But that's just his fun-loving spirit. That's what people like about him. He embraces the dork we all have inside of us.

—Stylist and friend John Dahlstrom

CHAPTER THIRTEEN

Aim for the High Notes

While *I was running* the YMCA camps, I was also working part-time at Brentwood, a local elementary school. I was helping out in the after-school program. One day, the principal of Brentwood, Linda McMasters, whom everyone called Dr. Mac, came to speak with me.

"I've been watching you run these programs," she said. "I've got a teacher who's going on maternity leave and I'd like for you to substitute while she's gone. Would you be willing to do that?"

She said she had a lot of faith in me as a teacher. That I was special.

I thought, *Really?*

She said, "Give it a try. If you hate it you can quit."

Dr. Mac was beautiful. She was very tall and thin, with silver hair in a side-parted bob. She had big glasses and always dressed in pantsuits. She was a brilliant and formidable woman. So when she asked me to teach, I said yes, even though I wasn't sure.

At the time, I was taking college courses in Raleigh, still pondering exactly what I should do with my life. I was nineteen and I knew I wanted to work with children, but I wasn't sure how.

What Dr. Mac didn't tell me was that my new class was a roomful of kids with autism.

—

My first day was a nightmare.

I got in there and discovered that I had a teacher's assistant who was miserable. She didn't want to be there, and she made this clear by refusing to do anything useful. In addition to her, I had a roomful of kids who displayed extremely different behavior characteristics and were in the process of freaking out because their routine had been disrupted.

I was not in the room ten minutes before one of the kids threw his shoes at me. Since it looked like fun, a few other kids tossed their shoes, too. One girl was so anxious she would not stop jabbering. She talked nonsense all day. Another little boy, named Lima, sat in the corner, staring into the middle distance. I asked Jesus, *What am I going to do with these kids?* I thought I wouldn't last a week.

But there was one child, who I'll call Mitch, who climbed into my heart.

—

Mitch anthropomorphized things. He would talk to the ceiling fan as if it were a real person. He likewise conversed with the copy machine and with the shredder.

When Mitch got upset he wasn't able to say what he needed, so he would pick the nearest heavy item and hurl it at your head. That was not fun, obviously, but learning how to communicate with him was. Mitch functioned at a high enough level, but many people couldn't tell. Once I began to learn how to comprehend what he needed, the hurling of heavy objects stopped. That felt like a true accomplishment.

After a time I could anticipate when he was growing distraught. I learned how to redirect him so he wouldn't get enraged anymore. I spent so many hours with him that I took the job home with me. Most of my free time was spent thinking about Mitch and the other children, wondering how I could help.

Mitch loved any type of electronic equipment or machinery. He also liked doing office work. When the office needed a bunch of stuff stapled, I let him sort and staple it. These were key lessons for him, because I wanted to teach him skills he could actually use later in life.

In the meantime, he was teaching me.

Kids with autism show you how to deal with humanity. No two children with autism are alike; they're all individuals—individuals to the extreme. So they teach you to see people as separate, rather than as part of a group with a set of expectations for that group.

They also teach you to have ridiculous amounts of patience.

And how to duck.

—

While the school searched for a new teacher, they hired a different substitute teacher every day. This doesn't work well for kids with autism. They have to have structure. So I said, "You know what, if you can't give me the same substitute every day, I would rather do it by myself."

Dr. Mac agreed. Her confidence in me in that classroom was staggering. When I made mistakes, she would patiently talk me through them. I think she saw me as a protégé.

She saw what I didn't yet: that I was born to teach special education.

She kept saying, "Will you go to college soon, please? You need to study this." I remember one time she brought someone from the North Carolina central special education office to meet me. She was like a tiger with a side of beef. She was not going to let it go.

For two months I was the only teacher in the class. On a typical day we worked at different stations—depending on the level of the student, that might be handwriting or math. We had some kids who read and some who were working on fine motor skills, such as picking up blocks and putting them inside a jar.

I got wise to each child's quirk. I knew when Mitch was going to be mad. I could tell when Phillip was going to cry. I knew what Evie was going to do when she was hungry.

With every day that passed, these kids became more compelling to me. There was something new in every class. Nothing ever remained static.

One of my students—let's call her Kyra—was fearless. She would fall down and crack her chin and not even notice it until she saw the blood. One day she was listening to the computer with headphones on that were bigger than her head. She kept saying in a quiet voice, "Mr. Clayton, it was a spider, it was a spider."

Autism produces conundrums. I kept trying to deconstruct what "spider" meant to Kyra. There was no spider on her video screen; there was no visual that even vaguely resembled an arachnid. About five minutes later, I looked at the floor and there was the largest spider I had ever seen. It was the size of a tarantula. I jumped onto the desk, but Kyra didn't flinch.

"Mr. Clayton, it was a big spider."

"Yes, Kyra," I said, "it was."

—

Kyra was advanced enough to go to the bathroom on her own, but she always lugged a trash can back. She'd come walking down the hallway dragging this giant Rubbermaid barrel behind her.

One day I decided to tie the trash can to the wall. Kyra left for her bathroom run and was gone a long time. I figured she was trying to untether the can.

A few minutes later, I spotted her walking down the hall with nothing but a shirt on. She had left her pants and panties in the bathroom with the trash can.

I ran to meet her, but she had already walked half-naked all the way down the hall, past the windows of every other grade school class. I was terrified that all the kids were going to stare and make fun of her. But not a single child did.

The teachers themselves were shocked. They expected the worst. But somehow not one child laughed. The only comment came from a second grader who said, "I hope Kyra gets her pants back."

I believe this was because of Dr. Mac. She created an atmosphere of tolerance and sensitivity. She made sure *all* the kids ate in the cafeteria. There were plenty of times when I would have preferred to stay in the classroom where I could keep an eye on the kids, but Dr. Mac said no. She made sure we *all* went to assemblies. Some of my students might scream or call out during the program, but so what? Dr. Mac wanted everyone to be there. "They are as much a part of this school as any other child," she explained.

Because of her policies, these kids were accepted.

Of course, the school had to hire a full-time teacher. Dr. Mac's confidence aside, I was still a nineteen-year-old with no formal training.

The school chose a woman named Tina Trent, who had very little experience with autism, but she did have a diverse special education background. She turned out to be amazing.

Within a month she had those kids doing things that I never thought they'd be able to do and excelling at skills I thought they'd never master. She even took some of them out of the room for part of the day. I'd found it so much easier to keep the kids in the classroom. It gave me a sense of control. But once Tina got there, she integrated them with the other kids.

She had Mary attend reading class. She took Ben to social studies. Now, they may not have been able to keep up exactly, their program may have been modified, but they were in the class with everybody else.

The results blew me away. The kids behaved so differently. They went from screeching in the middle of class to staying quiet. They stopped picking their noses and wiping it on somebody else. They stopped behaviors that they didn't see the other kids doing. They assimilated by themselves. It was breathtaking.

Tina believed that by putting the students in a classroom with kids who didn't have disabilities, she could help mainstream them. She introduced me to this whole idea of inclusion and the value of it for all the students.

I saw how kids without disabilities learn a lot from kids with them. For a start, they realize that there are more things to worry about than what to wear to school on Monday.

Until Tina got there, I thought I was pretty good in my class. I taught those children in that room for a month and a half, and nobody died. So I was proud of myself.

Then I saw what was possible. I saw what a difference being an exceptional teacher could make. Tina never made excuses—not for the kids, and not for herself. It was because of her that I initially had the idea that I could incorporate children with autism into the YMCA camps.

After working with Tina for a while I knew that I

wanted to be as good as she was. I didn't want to be a part-timer anymore. I was inspired to run my own class.

I told her, "I'm leaving next year. You've shown me what I was meant to do with my life. I'm going to teach special ed."

Dr. Mac couldn't have been happier. "There's a job waiting for you when you get done," she said, grinning.

—

If you had told me when I was a high school senior that in two years I'd wind up wanting to teach special-needs children, I'd have said you were nuts. But Tina and Dr. Mac changed my mind—about many things.

They showed me that if you make tolerance the norm, people adapt.

That if you institute policies of inclusion, inclusion becomes ordinary.

That when you are forced to rub elbows with people you might not automatically choose to, everyone benefits.

That hate is based on fear of the unknown, and fear dissipates with exposure. It evaporates like dew in the midday sun.

That when you believe in kids, they will never, ever let you down.

—

I was thrust into the special-education environment. I never knew I would enjoy it so much. I never thought I would be good at it. I never anticipated it would become my calling.

I have always believed in a life of service. But Tina, Dr. Mac, and the kids I worked with at Brentwood crystallized that desire. They helped me to see how vital it is for me to use my time on earth to make a difference in some way.

If it is by performing and touching someone's heart, great.

If it's being a teacher and helping some kid understand something, even better.

For now, I am happy using my voice as a means to an end. I'm learning how to wait. That's what happens when you work with kids.

Children with disabilities never tell you what they plan to throw at you. It could be a block, a brick, a live mouse. You have to be prepared for anything and grateful for the smallest progress. Whenever I feel adrift, I think back to the kids I used to teach.

Children in even the most devastating circumstances still smile.

They still laugh and reach out to others.

They still trust.

They still try.

Clay is wise for his years. I think he was raised right.
That's all I can figure.

—Sarge, tour bus driver who has chauffeured
David Bowie, 38 Special, Def Leppard,
and many other less well-mannered musicians

CHAPTER FOURTEEN

Understand What You're Singing For

I *left Brentwood* for college in Charlotte in 2000 and enrolled in the University of North Carolina special-education program. For an after-school job, I joined a government program that assigned teachers in training to a family with a child with a disability.

Mike Bubel was a twelve-year-old child with autism. I worked with him every week for a year and a half. Mike had a pretty typical childhood. Family vacations. Playgrounds. Amusement parks. However, because of his behavioral characteristics, he had avoided some outings that most of us see as routine activities.

Because of what I had learned from Tina, I thought maybe Mike should try some of the nonsocial outings that other kids took part in. I decided I was going to take him to places like the grocery store and the library. He could work on skills like paying for purchases and waiting for change.

Diane worried that he wouldn't be able to function well in social situations where he had defined responsibilities.

"Well, other teenagers have to do stuff they hate. It's a part of growing up. He might as well be miserable too," I joked. "And he may learn something in the process."

So we went places, and Mike loved it. He surpassed all my expectations.

It was on a trip to the Winn-Dixie, where I was letting him scan the items and hand over the money to the cashier, that I had an epiphany. I thought that if somebody like me was with Mike all the time, he could go to the YMCA camp with the other kids.

I still had not forgotten about Rene and all the other children with special needs who were being kept isolated and cut off from life for no supportable reason. I thought that since there are camp scholarship programs for kids who couldn't otherwise afford to go, why couldn't there be a program for kids with disabilities?

I convinced myself that after I graduated I would go back to the YMCA and institute a program that did just that. I didn't want to help kids one at a time. I wanted to make a large-scale change.

As God would have it, I was about to get my wish.

———

Diane Bubel had heard me singing around her house. She told me that she'd been watching this show called *American Idol* and that I should really consider applying for the next season.

I said, "I'm not really all about that stuff anymore."

But she kept on pestering me. "Just watch," she begged. "Watch it one time."

So I watched the show.

The next time I saw her, she told me she'd found out that they were preauditioning the next season in Charlotte. "You've got to go!" she urged.

"Okay, fine, I'll go," I replied.

I went. And I was cut.

Diane refused to give up. "Go to Atlanta and try again," she pleaded.

There was something about her insistence, her unquestioning belief in me, that made me feel I had to give it another try.

———

So I did, and I ended up staying on the show until the last episode.

Because of *American Idol,* I had to leave college six credit-hours shy of graduation. A professor suggested that I create a model nonprofit organization in order to accrue the final hours I needed.

The idea was to fabricate a mission statement for a cause that was not already part of a national group. I was to create a foundation and prepare a prospectus for it, something that detailed what it would take to get the nonprofit up and running—everything from fund-raising and grassroots efforts to arguing for legislation. I said, "Sure." After all, thanks to Mike Bubel, I already had an idea for something like this. So I set about making up a charity that addressed my concerns about inclusion and the YMCA.

Because I was excited about the idea, I mentioned the project in an interview or two when I was doing *American Idol* press. I called it the Bubel/Aiken Foundation.

Before long, I was getting checks from fans. I would get them through *American Idol* or, later, on the *Idol* tour. People would hand checks to ushers to take backstage. I was thinking, *What am I going to do with these? It's just a model for a foundation, people. It's not real!*

I was stressing about what to do with the money, when my friend Fran Skinner Lewis, who had done work with nonprofits before, suggested that I make the foundation legitimate. I'd already done all the prep. Why not bring it to life?

By the end of the *American Idol* tour, we had over $50,000 worth of donations. And the Bubel/Aiken Foundation was born.

———

The first thing I decided was that Fran should run Bubel/Aiken. I trusted her, and she already knew the ropes of nonprofit work. I told her, "Strategize all you want with the program, but our first task is to call the national headquarters of the YMCA." I wanted us to develop a partnership so we could go into these camp programs and make them available to all children.

We started with a YMCA in Kansas City, which agreed to be the pilot program. We said we would train their staff and provide our own supplementary staff, so they would have no reason not to try it. On top of that, we promised to buy the equipment for the whole camp. They were thrilled.

Encouraged, we approached the YMCA in Raleigh, where I used to work.

To my surprise and profound disappointment, they were not biting. I tried to explain that what I had in mind was for the foundation to train staff, provide additional help, even hire one staff member for each child if that was what it would take. But for reasons I still cannot understand, they were unwilling to work with us the way the YMCA in Kansas City had done. I wanted the YMCA to be open to all comers. From what I could see, they wanted only high-functioning kids.

For the past year, we've had fight after fight after fight, and we're still fighting with them. The battle has forced me to grow up a little. I am learning a new form of patience. Children with autism can be wearing, but trying to enlighten corporate America is far more maddening.

I'm not giving up, though.

Fate is a funny thing.

If I hadn't taught at the YMCA, I would never have met Dr. Mac, who would never have encouraged me to try special education, a goal without which I would never have left Raleigh and never met Diane and Mike Bubel, and certainly would not have auditioned for *American Idol,* which turned out to be the most significant event in my life to date.

I named my foundation after Mike because it was at his house that the two parts of my life converged: music and children.

Meeting that family was one of those rare moments of alchemy that spring up in your life and alter it forever. By creating the Bubel/Aiken Foundation, I ensured that the moment wouldn't pass.

The foundation is my future now. I feel that speaking out for others is the best way to use my voice—the rest of it, all the pop-star stuff, is ultimately a platform for giving back. And I have come too far to give up now. Resistance will not deter me from what I intend to do, from what I see as my higher purpose.

I was planning to teach in the classroom. I am still teaching. My classroom has just gotten a lot bigger.

I don't think Clayton ever had it in his heart to be a star. I think he really just wanted to help people, to work with people in need, so the focus would not be on him. Performing was more of a hobby on the side. And when he went on *American Idol* I remember him saying, "If I make the final thirty-two, that would be great." And then, "If I make it to the final twelve." And on it went. He never once talked about wanting to win. He was just really happy with each step.

—**Mary Propes, high school social studies teacher and family friend**

CHAPTER FIFTEEN

Sing Your Own Song

I *didn't win* on *American Idol.*

In the beginning, I didn't even make it past the final thirty-two. I was cut—which, I have to say, was a good eye-opener for me.

Back home, I had been singing in competitions since I was a little boy. And I was used to winning them. I think I probably had the potential to be really overconfident. I don't want to say I was cocky, but I had some experience with talent shows, and I was comfortable competing. Not that it was that difficult.

First of all, in the South, where I am from, not many guys sing. I was usually the best guy singer in the room. It wasn't like football, which every guy played. When there are only three boys singing within a three-hundred-mile radius, your odds of winning a contest are pretty good.

I also sang a lot in church, which is an awfully generous audience. If you sing in church, you get the idea that you have a decent voice—even if you don't.

—

When I initially auditioned for *American Idol* in Charlotte, I didn't even make it past the screeners. I thought, *Are you kidding me?* I was genuinely surprised.

I have a stubborn streak, so when Diane urged me to go to the auditions in Atlanta, I drove myself down there, ready to try again.

I was ill prepared for the talent pool. In fact, I was shocked. I had never been in a place where so many people were so good at singing. It was a nice little kick in the butt. It put a bit of the fear of God in me.

I got up there with the other contestants and thought, *Oh my goodness, I may be good, I may be decent, but that girl or boy can sing*. It was a reality check. I was not in Raleigh anymore.

Not only that, but it quickly became apparent that I did not look like the other kids who were trying out.

—

Looking back, I think my differences—I wasn't traditionally handsome, I didn't (and don't) resemble Nick Lachey, I have no pecs to speak of—are what secured me a spot in Hollywood. Randy Jackson and Simon Cowell found the combination of my appearance and my voice intriguing.

"Where is that voice coming from?" they kept asking at the first audition.

"You don't look like a pop star," Cowell said, leaning back in his chair. "Now what?"

If I had looked the part, maybe I wouldn't have stuck in their minds. If I had been the same as every other boy who tried out, I would have been easier to forget. But a skinny, bespectacled redhead with lung power—that they remembered. It was my very oddness that made me special. And this time, it was special in a good way.

Timing was everything.

I was twenty-four years old and had finally pulled away from focusing on pleasing others. It's ironic in so many ways. I spent my entire grade school, middle school, and high school careers attempting to fit in and make friends. I was a master of ingratiation. And then I got to *American Idol,* and it was the first time in my life that I really relaxed and began celebrating my talent for standing out.

—

At the start of the competition, I was in the group with Ruben Studdard and Kimberley Locke. There were four groups of eight, and the top two out of each group of eight went on to be in the finals.

In my group I took third place, behind Kim and Ruben. Only two contestants can make it through and I was not one of them, so I was sent packing.

At the time, I was annoyed about that. The executive producer of the show, Nigel Lythgoe, warned me that the closer I got to making the top dozen, the more painful it would be to lose. His theory was borne out.

I knew there were going to be wild-card slots, and a few *Idol* staff members had told me that the odds were good that I'd be invited back. The idea was that nine of us who had been cut would be offered a second chance to compete.

I wasn't going to take any chances. At the first opportunity I had after the last two finalists were picked, I called the show. I wanted to know what was happening. Would I be returning to audition again?

After some badgering, I was told I would have one of the wild-card slots. I was thrilled.

A few weeks later, I was back at the *American Idol* set. I sang "Don't Let the Sun Go Down on

Me." Simon said he was impressed. America agreed and chose me to fill the wild-card slot.

—

I was overjoyed—and grateful. But I didn't envision myself becoming a superstar.

I never expected to win the title. I kept saying, "If I just make it to the next level, that will be enough." And it would have been enough. I was happy for my family just to have been given the opportunity to see me on television.

My mom always stressed that you didn't have to win to succeed. She'd say, "Look at Lucille Ball. She was told she had no talent. Michael Jordan was cut from his high school basketball team."

So every time I got a chance to go onstage and sing, I was prepared for it to be the last. I would even call my friends and warn them that I was going home.

When I survived week to week, when the people watching at home voted me in—that validation moved me profoundly. It was as if all the kids like me, those who had been teased or ostracized or abandoned, saw a little part of themselves in me. I was more popular than I ever dreamed I would be. It felt a little bit like the revenge of the nerds.

During the run of the show, I began to get calls from people I had known in school who had never even spoken to me before—people who had ignored me or gossiped about me in the locker room, people who would not have spit in my mouth if my teeth were on fire. Now they were calling me, my mama, and my actual friends and talking about how close we had been back in the day. All I could do was laugh.

I had tried and failed for twelve years to be the same as everyone else and I realized that I was *never* going to convince anyone that I was cool. I was content not to blend. I had made an uneasy peace with this.

Now, I won't say I wasn't nervous when I saw all these attractive, hip kids I was competing against. I had no reason to think I would be rewarded for my choice to be my own geek.

But, miraculously, I was.

—

The best thing about being on *American Idol* was the life education it gave me. There is no school for pop stars. But *American Idol* was boot camp. And if there is one thing boot camp is designed to do, it's to prepare you for anything.

I learned so much—not just how to perform onstage and do the press, but how to negotiate with all the different types of people who are in the business—really nice people like Kim Locke, really sweet and innocent people like Carmen Rasmusen, people who are savvy and know their business like Ruben Studdard, people who are in it only for themselves like some folks I won't mention.

Living in the *Idol* mansion really opened my eyes. Outside of the obvious differences, all of the finalists in the house had very strong personalities, which is the reason we were on that show. No weak personality would have made it that far.

Everybody's got flaws. But people whose personalities were pronounced were the people who stayed around. This kept things interesting, especially in the house.

We had some divas. We had some cheerleaders. We had some snobs. In a way, it was like high school all over again. Only this time, everyone sang. Singing wasn't this unusual little interest that set us apart; it was what we shared.

Most people in the house thought I was a square. I didn't drink or smoke or swear. I was Sandra Dee.

I believed that since America had voted to put me there, I had a responsibility to make the most of it. So I made a plan.

———

My goal was twofold.

First, I was determined to stay realistic. I never anticipated winning (which is good, seeing as I didn't). I knew that no matter what happened, good or bad, it was not going to last forever. I was going to end up being a teacher, so I maintained a pretty tight grip on reality. I was on *American Idol* to compete, but I told myself that it wasn't going to be the end of the world if I lost.

Second, I wanted to savor the experience. I wanted to use the show as a chance to learn. So I made sure I was always prepared—prepared to be booted, prepared to perform, prepared to do my best.

I have always taken performing pretty seriously. When you see people entertain and they're enjoying it, you can tell. I'm fairly observant, and when I watch other singers onstage, I take notes.

When I was in middle school, I saw a lot of singers who had solos and they'd just stand there and sing. They might've sounded fine, but you could tell they were nervous. They were so worried, they forgot about the audience. They didn't engage. I remember even back then thinking about how I didn't want my solos to look that way. I wanted to be sure to interact with the crowd.

So I'd practice. Every time I had to sing in church I'd sing in front of the mirror first. I'd pretend I had a microphone and I would act big! I'd sing looking up, imagining there were rafters or that people were in the stands. This wasn't the case, of course. My church was about the size of the tour bus. But I'd always look skyward and move my arms and tilt my head. I'd do all this over-the-top prep work.

I figured that when it was my turn to sing I'd just go up there and do my thing. I might look like a fool, but at least the crowd wouldn't be bored.

On *American Idol* I told myself, *I'm going to work my butt off every week; I'm going to learn my songs, and when I have time, I'm going to make friends.* And that's what I did. And that's what Ruben did, too. There were other people who approached the show as a great opportunity to hang out and have fun. They would party at night and sleep late—and end up getting cut early.

Every week I picked my song by choosing the first thing that came into my head. And every week I would second-guess myself. Then I'd say, *No, you can't second-guess yourself; you need to stick with what you know.*

The songs I picked were songs I'd already memorized. I could have tried to learn something new and show off, but there was no point in that. As my mom would say, there's never a good reason to toot your own horn.

—

My plan was working wonderfully until the night I decided to sing "Grease."

The judges had been telling me that I needed to mix it up. They were urging me to take more chances with my song selections. The time had come to be bold.

I remember rehearsing that song and asking everyone to clear out of the room so I could practice the dancing. The vocal coach, Debra Byrd, stayed and said, "Now, you know you're going to have to move on this."

And I said, "I know, I know."

And we came up with the hip thing. I knew I was going to feel like a fool, but she said, "Just do it!" So I did.

I sang "Grease." I wore a fitted red leather jacket and snug pants. I strutted around the stage. And at the right moment, I smiled and ticked my hips back and forth in a desperate effort to extend my capabilities.

Simon's eyes could not have rolled more dramatically if they'd fallen from their sockets onto an ice rink. He said the performance was horrible. He mocked my outfit and my pitiful attempt at dancing.

I have never pretended I can dance because, obviously, I can't. And I think when I did, people were stunned. There was a feeling of shock in the audience. It was the equivalent of my pulling my pants down in public.

I was teased about that jacket for the rest of the show and long into the *American Idol* tour. My mother wears it now. It looks far better on her.

Still, even though I took a lot of flak for the stilted hip thrusts and the bad fashion selection, I was able to laugh it off. The song was my choice and I did the best job I knew how.

When you can say with confidence that you gave your best, there is really no point in beating yourself up after the fact. I learned that when you try your best, you can't really feel that bad when you fail. And the more you laugh at yourself, the less it hurts when someone else does it.

For example, during *American Idol,* Simon kept saying I didn't look the part. That was his only comment: "You don't look like a pop star." So midway through the series, in my interview for the next package to introduce me, I decided I was going to crack on myself before Simon got a chance. I thought I should pinpoint something. Simon has no idea what he's picking on. He was not going to straight-up tell me, "You're ugly."

So on the tape I said, "I can work to improve my singing, but"—I grabbed my ears—"I'm always going to have these."

I put my aesthetic deficiencies on the table so that Simon couldn't comment on them anymore. Simon wants to be original. He doesn't want to be repeating something somebody already said. And I said it directly: "I know I look weird; I don't care."

So what did Simon say that night? He said, "You know what, you may not look like a pop star, but I think that's what makes you so special."

Gotcha!

—

I have been told that many of the people watching *American Idol* thought I seemed professional. They would call my mom and tell her how calm I looked on the air. Friends e-mailed me to say I didn't look at all nervous.

I don't think I was such a pro. I think I was organized. Not that I was prepared for what that show would do for my life, but I was ready for how I was going to handle it.

I mentally rehearsed. I knew how I was going to respond when Simon cracked on me. I was primed for him to say something mean—that's why I never commented back to him. That, and because it's tacky to talk back.

Since I was ready, my face never betrayed any surprise or shock when he was nasty. I think that's why people thought I looked so confident. Not because I was necessarily confident, because, believe me, I had questions, I had doubts. But I was ready for bad news if it came.

Starting from the moment I walked into the Atlanta audition, I was fully prepared for Simon to say something mean. I told myself, *Let me just go in here, do my thing and be ready for him to say something cruel and tell me to go home, that I would not be coming to Hollywood.*

I was very pleasantly surprised when he said, "Come on down."

—

The truth is, I have a real fear of looking like an idiot—an intrinsic, disproportionate fear.

I think it's because, as I mentioned, I spent a lot of my middle school years being the brunt of a joke or two. I was picked on, and I made up my mind even then that I wasn't going to let them see me upset. I wasn't going to let those bullies see me cry. When it comes to hurting people, Simon had nothing on the kids at school.

I'm still ready for the worst. Every single time I go onstage, I'm prepared for the crowd to boo me.

Now, what are the chances that they're going to boo me? They've bought tickets. They probably like the way I sing. And yet if I am to be booed, I don't want to be shocked. I don't want to be hurt. I don't want to show someone that they upset me.

I guess that comes from my mother. She was always ready for whatever anyone had to say. She was nothing if not resilient.

I admire people who are ready for anything. Basically, I don't like surprises; in fact, I hate surprises. A surprise party? I don't want that. Uh-uh. Because I will not be prepared for that.

I don't like being embarrassed. I don't like being

caught off guard. It reminds me of the times that I wasn't quick enough to respond when somebody picked on me. It reminds me of a time in my life when I was vulnerable.

When you're a kid and your life is uncertain, you adapt. In my early years, I lived in fear, wondering what was going to happen next. Those experiences instilled in me a need for order. I need to be equipped for anything.

So now I like to know what's coming. Because really, who wants to be laughed at? Who wants to be booed?

Let's say I did a show and someone booed me. I think I would just keep singing. I'd sing louder. I would keep going, I would persevere, and, hopefully, people would think, *That dude, he did his stuff. He didn't break; he didn't crack; he was very mature; he was very professional. He got up there and he sang.*

———

During the filming of the show, those of us who were involved thought it was a cult hit, but we never had any inkling of just how pervasive *American Idol* was. The only clue I got was when they assigned me a bodyguard for my trip home.

We went to Raleigh to tape bits for the last shows. While there, we were overwhelmed. I was chased. People shrieked. I was completely freaked out because not only had I never been chased, but I had no idea how many people were actually watching the program.

Suddenly there were seventy thousand people in a stadium to hear me sing the national anthem. That was stunning.

I remember that when the third *American Idol* was airing, I would watch all the coverage in disbelief. It was on CNN, Nickelodeon, Fox, PBS. You couldn't flip on the television without somebody talking about *American Idol.*

I asked my friends whether the show had been that popular the season I was singing, and they said, "More."

I guess I had no idea how much of an impact the program had on the culture. I just know how much of an impact it had on me.

—

Because of American Idol, I finally realized that it's okay to be different as long as I'm proud of my differences. If strangers were proud of me, then why the heck couldn't I be proud of myself?

I never knew where my social place was in the world, but America found room for me. That felt nice. It helped me to realize that it's not so important how you look or what you wear. What's important is being happy with yourself.

That I had this insight on a national television

show is hilarious—because, really, when are looks more important than when you are being watched by ten million viewers a week?

I suppose I had been obsessed with my flaws for so long that by the time I appeared on *American Idol,* I was over it. And when those calls began coming in, it was like a thousand voices saying, "You're right. Looks don't matter. Self-respect does."

Thanks to the viewers, it grew easier not to care. Being myself was working. People liked me for me.

It sounds small, but it was one of the biggest realizations of my life. And I have strangers to thank for it.

And Simon, of course.

Women want to hug anyone associated with Clay Aiken. The bus driver. The manager. Even me. I was out the other night and all these women saw I was wearing a Clay Aiken Tour laminate. They pounced on me. They are truly fanatics. I've never seen anything like it.

—Bob Davis, tour accountant who has toured with Metallica, BBMak, and many others

CHAPTER SIXTEEN

Make Sure the Audience Can Sing Along

My *fans are unlike* any other fans in the world. To start, they are maternal. They worry about me. They notice if I look tired on a talk show. They send flowers when they find out that my dog, Raleigh, has been to the vet. They bake me brownies and batches of peanut butter fudge. They also send me hand-embroidered underwear, but more often than not, this is of the "granny" variety.

My fans are loyal and kind and prone to singing along. There are a few fans who tell me they think I'm perfect. To them I say, "Your standards are too low."

There are, of course, those fans who go too far—

like the ones who throw themselves at the tour bus. Or the ones who drive behind us for eight hours and try to snag an autograph when we stop at the gas station at four in the morning. Then there is this one woman who swears that she is deaf, but when I sing she can hear me. I think that is a little unfathomable. My mother, of course, believes her.

—

I'm different, which is why I think my fans are different. As pop singers go, I am about as non-threatening as you can get. I'm not going to take advantage of anyone's daughter. I'm not going to be found passed out in an elevator somewhere. I'm not a player by anyone's definition.

I am also more of a television personality than a radio presence. John Mayer, Michelle Branch—people know them when they hear them, but they may not recognize them when they're walking down the street. I'm known for what I achieved on television, so for better or worse, everyone knows what I look like.

I am grateful for this attention. I know that people have spent money to come hear me sing, and that amazes me. I still find the whole phenomenon of fame unnerving. Being mobbed is a strange feeling, especially since I'm uncomfortable in big groups.

This year I was lucky enough to participate in *A Capitol Fourth* for PBS, a televised musical Independence Day celebration that took place in Washington, D.C. There was a swanky reception for the artists afterward in the Capitol building. I went to this reception, but the moment I walked in and saw all the people there, I began to sweat. My heart raced. I knew no one intended to do me harm, but I felt paranoid. I was terrified. Vince Gill was there shaking hands. Barry Bostwick was chatting with people and being friendly. I wanted to crawl under a statue. I felt backed into a corner.

I think it's because in my life before *American Idol*, I was never viewed as attractive to other people. No one was interested in me. I moved through the world largely unnoticed. And now all of a sudden, I can't leave my house without someone snapping a picture.

Maybe if fame were something I had chased, something I desired, then this attention would make sense to me. But for someone planning to become a high school principal becoming a pop star instead is unsettling.

—

My mother says fans like me because of what I represent. I'm not sure what that means.

I've had fans tell me I'm an angel, or a saint. This always makes me chuckle. Nobody is a saint, and if I had a halo it would be crooked.

If anything, I represent the nerd who made good.

I'm not an unobtainable sex symbol like Justin Timberlake. And I think my fans appreciate that.

I know it's not a popular idea, but I take being a role model very seriously. I know how much kids pay attention to so-called celebrities. If I happen to be someone they look up to, I want to be sure I am worthy of emulation. That has been a goal of mine my whole life and has only become more critical now. The exposure has taken some getting used to.

The first time I realized that what I did mattered to a larger audience was during a meet and greet at a radio station in Atlanta. A woman approached me, and she was sobbing.

She said, "I just wanted to let you know how much your video for 'Invisible' changed my life."

And I said, "Really?" I mean, it's a pretty narcissistic video. I said, "It's just me onstage with a bunch of people screaming for me."

I was kidding with her. She was crying, and I wanted to help her laugh a little. And then she said, "I used to weigh two hundred and fifty pounds. And I hated myself for so long. And it meant so much to me to see that you had an overweight girl in your video."

I had to think about it, because I didn't remember any overweight girls in the video. She told me she meant the girl who climbed onstage as I sang to her.

Then I remembered the girl. I remembered her because she was from New Jersey and was visiting L.A. for her birthday. She came to California because she heard I was going to be on Jay Leno's show, and she just happened to be riding the bus past the site of the video shoot. She hopped off the bus and cheered and clapped so loudly that the director decided it would be fun to put her up onstage.

Her weight never crossed my mind. She was a normal girl. But her being normal and being in a video had brought on a wave of comfort for this woman in Atlanta.

"I wish I had seen a video like that when I was younger," she explained. "It would have saved me a world of hurt. I only hope that some other heavy girls watched it and realized they don't have to look like rail-thin models. They don't have to hate themselves."

For weeks I thought about what that woman had said to me. She didn't know it, but she had given me a new sense of what I might be able to accomplish.

—

When I cast my next video, for "The Way," I told the producers that I wanted to use everyday people. I had images I hoped to use: an older couple grocery shopping and still being playful with each other, geeky boys with pretty girls, chunky girls with jocks. I wanted to show these couples in love, not all sexed up and grinding on the hood of an Escalade.

I thought I had made myself clear, but when the day came to shoot I saw that the kids they had cast were awfully attractive. I pulled the video commissioner from RCA aside and asked, "What happened?"

He argued that the kids were exactly what I had asked for. "They're multicultural," he said. "They're quirky."

I tried to explain that quirky is not the same as geeky. Quirky happens when kids feel so confident and accepted that they can consciously differentiate themselves. Geeky happens when kids are clueless.

I gave him an example from my own life in middle school, when I was the last person to realize that carrying your backpack with two straps was uncool. Nobody told me, and I wasn't swift enough to figure it out on my own. And then, naturally, I kept one-strapping it way past the time when it was the thing to do. I was hopeless.

I wanted kids in my video who were two-strappers. Kids whose pants were too short, whose hair was the wrong style, who had braces and cheap shoes, who felt out of place and at a loss as to how to fix it.

The commissioner thought I was nuts. Who wants to watch a video about losers?

I argued that the messages we put out there matter to people. That we should take a lot more care in making certain that what we're showing is positive and encouraging. That I never need to see another video with a pretty young girl dressed like a hooker. And then I reminded him that until a couple years ago I was considered a loser.

He said he'd do his best.

In the end, I lost the battle. The final cut of the video showcases a cast of beautiful people whose beauty is moderately downplayed. The only exception is a boy in a pool hall who is doted on by a gorgeous girl. I told the producers that I wouldn't show up for filming if they didn't cast him, so they did.

When I watch that video now, I am thankful that he's in it. The boy and girl in that scene look sweet and real and genuinely in love. The images resonate with me because I was that guy. I understand people who feel out of place. And maybe some other young man will watch it and think, *Hey, he's not perfect, but he got the girl anyway.*

—

I am indebted to my fans for so many things. Their support. Their care. Their peanut butter fudge. Even the underwear they send me.

I am thankful mainly that they continue to teach me what counts. My fans show me a better way to use my fame. My fans keep me real.

If I'd had them in school, I never would have been a two-strapper.

I think being a star has changed Clay for the better. His confidence level has gone up. Before he wouldn't be as willing to stand up for himself. Now he worries a lot less about trying to be somebody else. I know he won't live a life that other people want him to live. He may up and decide to quit and go back to teaching. I don't think he'd have a second thought about leaving the entertainment life.

—Nick Leisey

CHAPTER SEVENTEEN

Don't Sing Rock If You Really Are a Balladeer

I *learned from my* birth father that the one thing you can count on in life is that your life is going to change.

Everyone grows and transforms. You might become something you never expected you'd be. Being a pop star was never a dream I had for myself. But God had other plans. I am learning to acknowledge that.

I used to be far more stubborn. I remember one time in high school when I got into an argument with my mom at dinner. She wanted me to eat some pork dish she had made. I refused. And she said, "The only way you're not going to have to eat that dinner is if you're a vegetarian."

Now, I loved meat. I ate hamburgers all the time. But because she challenged me, I snottily announced that I was, in fact, a vegetarian. And here's the stubborn part—I didn't eat meat for two years.

After that, God must have decided I needed to learn a few more lessons, because since then, whatever life plan I thought was going to happen bit the dust. I can accept that.

Accepting Los Angeles is harder.

—

A few years back, I was afraid to go to college in Charlotte.

My friend Nick said, "You need to leave the house. You need to leave your mama."

This was true. But college was two hours away.

I grew up with the notion that the sun rises over the ocean. When I moved to L.A. and someone suggested we watch the sun *set* over the ocean, I was confused. That's how cloistered I was. In my mind, California was like another planet.

Before I moved to L.A., I had never lived in a place where you couldn't speak your mind. In Raleigh, I could (and did) run my mouth. But in L.A., I need to be careful about what I say.

Many people who move to L.A. do so to get ahead. People live in big cities to climb a ladder. The South couldn't be more different. You don't move to Raleigh to climb ladders. You move there to sit in the wading pool. It's a slowerpaced life. That's why I like small towns. I like people not having an M.O. It seems to me that L.A. is all about what someone else can do for you. Nobody is out to get anything from anybody in Raleigh.

L.A. can be fun, but it is impossible to know what's real. The town is full of actors, and sometimes that carries over into real life. I prefer hanging out with people who worry less about what they're getting and more about what they're giving.

I know that L.A. has changed me. I have always been the type of person who gave people my trust until they showed me they didn't deserve it, but now I am the type of person who often doesn't trust someone until they prove to me that I can. I learned the hard way. People I believed in turned out to be deceiving me. It was a lesson I needed to get through my head. I am not as naive as I once was.

And that's a good thing. I needed to grow up. I needed a kick in the butt to stay vigilant.

Hollywood can be seductive. I can see how it's easy to get carried away by the glamour of the place. I'm afraid of becoming too occupied by what I am doing here, of unintentionally ignoring the people who matter back home, alienating the people who genuinely care about me, and then having my career end and not being worth anything to anyone. Everybody peaks at some point. Then what?

My mom always told me, "Don't get too big for your britches."

I bear that in mind.

—

Fame was not something that I had forecast in my life.

I remember sitting on the curb in Atlanta, waiting to audition for *American Idol,* and all these other boys and girls were telling me how they were "going to make it!"

"You'll see my name in lights someday," they said. "I am going to be a star!"

I feel a little guilty remembering that. Being famous was never anything I pursued. At the time, that wasn't such an issue, but as I progressed in the *American Idol* competition I began to feel like I had stolen someone's spot.

There are thousands of people who sing as well if not better than I do. But for some reason, here I am. People always say, "There is just something special about your voice. A quality."

I don't agree. I hear so many voices that are remarkable to me. Rickey Smith from *American Idol* has one of the most beautiful voices I have ever encountered. Quiana Parler, who is in my band, is amazing. She should have a record deal. Kimberley Locke's single is far better than mine—and she works harder.

I sometimes feel like an interloper in this industry because, in my heart, I wasn't even sure I wanted to be a singer. I was more interested in helping children. That was where my passion was, and still is.

God gave me this gift, this voice, and I am thankful for it. But I never honestly thought my voice was going to be the way I would make my living. I didn't even consider attending a performing arts college. I told my mom, "I'm not going to Nashville and knock on doors."

Because of that, I remind myself that I need to make the most of my opportunities. I need to use this ability to help others, not just to buy myself a new car.

—

Just recently I was watching an episode of *The West Wing,* my favorite show. On the program, the president was in a movie theater with his daughter. He kept narrating the film, chatting and interrupting, until his daughter finally said, "Dad, people are trying to watch the film."

And he said, "What do you want to bet that no one in here is going to shush me?"

When I saw that, I had this feeling of recognition. I'm in a place now where I could misbehave or act selfishly and no one would shush me. If I'm going to remain a decent human being, it's really up to me.

I remember when I had just started the *Idol* tour. It was my day off, and my bodyguard, Jerome, and I flew back to L.A. for a day to shoot the video for "This Is the Night." It was the first time that I had ever done anything where everyone catered to me. There were teams of people telling me what to wear, where I would stand, what I would do, mussing my hair. There was very little input from me. And I felt so uncomfortable. I had no control. It was beyond weird to see sixty people running around. It reminded me of one of those movie shots where one person is sitting still and the camera swirls around, recording chaos. That's how I felt. I was the eye of the storm. Little did I know there was a hurricane coming.

The *Idol* tour sold out in fifty-five cities.

Measure of a Man was released in October and went double platinum the first week.

In November I won the Fan's Choice Award at the American Music Awards.

I was a guest on *Good Morning America*. Letterman. Leno.

Then, on December 10, 2003, I was invited to perform "Invisible" at the *Billboard* Awards in Las Vegas. I decided to ask my mother to join me. It was the first time she had ever come to a major event since the *Idol* finale.

I remember we were in my trailer and the usual assortment of managers, stylists, and producers was also in the trailer, swarming around. I was getting my hair ironed into shape when I glanced over at my mother. She was wearing a black beaded dress and dinner jacket, and she was sitting quietly on a chair with her legs crossed at the ankles. It occurred to me that she seemed like a stranger. She didn't belong. And then I thought, I am a stranger here, too. I don't belong, either.

The event began, and my mother and I were seated in the front row. I was immediately sorry that I had invited her to come.

The show was crass. Dave Grohl made vulgar jokes. Paris Hilton and Nicole Richie said the "F" word. Nick Lachey and Jessica Simpson alluded to their sex life any chance they could. My mother stiffened. She winced. She was not enjoying what she would later call a "smutty little program."

The most peculiar moment came when I went backstage to perform. I looked out into the crowd, and there—sitting next to Beyoncé and her immense bodyguard—was my mother, grimacing.

If I could have left, grabbed my mom, and hightailed it to a Cracker Barrel, I probably would have.

—

Fame changes everything. I've figured out that now the people who care about me the most are the people who don't call me anymore. They check up on me now and again, but they aren't calling every week, asking me to hang out. The people doing that

are people who never would have deigned to social-
ize with me before. There are a lot of fair-weather
friendships going on.

It's hard to know who means well and who
doesn't. It makes it all the more important that you
stay true to yourself.

For example, during my first major meeting
about my album, Clive Davis and I talked about the
title of the record. He wanted to call it *Clay Aiken*.
I didn't. I felt that the songs on the album, good as
they are, didn't define me. I didn't choose them;
Clive did. And if a record was going to have my
name on the outside, I wanted it to be a project that
I had orchestrated. I told Clive I preferred the title
Measure of a Man, because it was a reminder of
why I'm here and what I said I wanted to do.

Clive was not pleased. Clive Davis is the emperor
of the recording industry in this country, and I
think I had irritated him.

He swiveled around in his chair. He looked out
his window onto the streets of New York City. "I
know it must be very intimidating to have me here
in the room with you," he said, smoothing out his
black turtleneck. "I don't want you to feel that way.
But you must understand."

My face began to flush.

While he was talking, telling me not to be nervous but at the same time trying to convince me I
was wrong, I heard my mother's voice in my head:
This is what you said you wanted to do. Don't you

back down on it. Don't you give in to somebody who is trying to make you into something that you don't want to be.

So I didn't.

I thought of my mother, and how she was never afraid of anybody.

I thought about her independence.

I thought about how she is nothing if not hospitable to everybody, even those people who are trying to change her mind.

And I said, "Mr. Davis, I respectfully decline to change the title of the album."

And you know what? He came around.

—

Since that time I've gotten more used to the interviews and the cameras. I know I am a part of this now. But it is such a huge departure. I have so much uncertainty. Will I still be doing this in five years?

When this ride is over, I won't stay in L.A. I'll go back to Raleigh. That is my plan, and I am ready for it.

But I wonder: What will happen to all the people I know in Hollywood? What happens to this life when I leave? Will it all be some distant memory? Or if I stay, if this remains my life, will the people I grew up with, the people who supported me and shaped me, vanish from my life?

Just recently, on tour at a show in Greensboro,

North Carolina, I pulled a woman onstage to dance with me. We had both been in Mrs. Norton's voice class when I was in eighth grade. It was the oddest coincidence.

I was singing "When You Say You Love Me," and I just happened to spy her in the front section, dancing. I called her up. She was delighted. She gave me a hug and whispered in my ear, "I miss you so much."

I was caught off guard. My past was intersecting with my new life. I ended up treating her like a fan. I hammed it up, and we danced. I smiled big.

I did this mainly because I didn't want to be embarrassed. I didn't want to start crying in front of seven thousand people. I felt off kilter. She was a living reminder of the old me.

I missed her, too. I missed my old life.

The song ended, and she got offstage and rejoined the crowd. At the end of the night she went home to her world, and I got back on the tour bus and drove to the next show.

———

Mom asked me, after *American Idol,* "Are you sure you want to be a singer? Because you'll be on the road half the year and you won't get to see your friends. It could be lonely."

But I enjoy touring.

L.A. is a sprawl of a city, and it has its charms.

But I like visiting smaller towns. New York City is great in limited doses, but I prefer seeing places like Lexington, Kentucky, and Kansas City, Missouri, and St. Paul, Minnesota.

To me, those places are the real world. When you live in Los Angeles or New York, you can get caught up in the pace and energy of those cities and start thinking that rushing and achieving are what life is all about.

I'd rather spend time with more grounded people, like the folks back in Raleigh. I can relate to them better. Small towns are welcoming to me. I can relax and be myself. It takes the pressure off.

There are people in Omaha, Nebraska, who have not been to the ocean. I know how that is. I had barely been anywhere outside of North Carolina before *American Idol*.

On my last tour I intentionally chose smaller cities and towns. I had played bigger, urban venues before, and they were gratifying. But there was just something about the level of enthusiasm in these smaller towns that was contagious.

I get excited when I see somebody else happy. Smalltown fans are thrilled when I drive out and wave from the bus. They will wait outside—sometimes for hours, sometimes in miserable weather—just to see me greet them. It can be a wild scene. Lots of shrieking. Girls trembling and weeping. My friend John finds it all a bit unnerving.

But I love seeing people joyful. It's great to witness the effects of the music. It makes that long drive to the next city that much easier when I know that it will matter to people that I am coming to sing.

———

I know that I am living the American dream. I am able to do something I enjoy and be recognized for that contribution.

I didn't always want to do this, but now that I am, it's exciting. I came out of a place that didn't provide these types of experiences and opportunities, but I've found that it doesn't matter where you grow up; if you can dream it, you can achieve it.

As long as people care enough about seeing me live, I will sing live. As long as we're able to do a positive show and keep people entertained, I'm ready to tour.

I was performing just the other night and I looked out and I saw this sea of cheery, singing faces. I heard their voices ringing, a giant swell of sound.

I said to myself, *That's acceptance, you know. That is one big hello.*

———

When we were in Charleston, South Carolina, we invited a girl onstage and asked her if she wanted to sing with me. She jumped up and down and said she wanted to sing "Without You," the duet I do with Kimberley Locke on her album.

This girl knew every word to the whole song. She knew the harmony. I sang with her, and I thought to myself, *You know, there were so many times in my life when all I wanted was to sing with Martina McBride.* I thought it would be so cool to get to perform a duet with her. And I said to myself, *I wonder if I'm making this young girl's day as much as it would've made mine to sing with Martina McBride.*

When she finished and left the stage, her friends circled her, jumping and squealing. My heart swelled. It moved me just to know that there are people out there who have bothered to memorize my songs. To me, that's unbelievable.

I am still surprised when people in the crowd sing along. Once on the last tour as we were playing "Measure of a Man," I had to stop singing for a second to clear my throat. I went quiet, but the whole audience kept singing the words. I stopped and listened to them. Then my eyes welled up. I was almost light-headed. I had to grab my backup singer's hand to steady myself because I thought, *There are fifteen thousand people in this room and they all know this song! They're all singing my song. Which means they listen to my song in their cars. I'm in their cars! I'm in their houses!*

It was one of those times when my new life washed over me, when I felt the power of music. It was almost too much.

My mother has always stressed the value of personal responsibility. That mandate takes on a whole new weight when fifteen thousand people are straining to hear every word you say, when they are committing your words to memory. It makes me think that I had better be selective about what comes out of my mouth.

I also worry about the kids in the audience. When I tour, it hits home that people have spent their money not just on a $15 CD, but also on a $45 ticket. Sometimes onstage I'll do the math: $45 dollars for a family of four—that's $200 once you've included tax; add $10 to park and $20 for Ticketmaster fees, plus if you buy a T-shirt that's another $30. People are paying some money.

I used to pick up the couch cushion to find change for gas, so I know the value of a dollar. That people would pay, that they would save up money just to see me—that's really flattering.

That's why I am committed to staying the least expensive tour in the country. Our priciest seat is $45. Madonna's go for more than $300. Good for her, but I hope my tour tickets will always be cheap.

I want to stay affordable because I want to fill the house. I'd rather fill the house than make a lot of money.

I want Mama to be able to bring her three kids and her sister. I want Grandma to be there, too. We do a family show. And as such, the entire family should be able to afford to attend.

It is important to me that we do something that I can be proud of and that you can afford to bring your kids to. I don't ever want my concert to cause someone to skip lunch for three months just so that they can go to the event. Live music should be available to everyone, not just the few with money.

—

During my last tour we pulled up to a truck stop in Pennsylvania at around three in the morning. I hadn't eaten after the show, and I was hungry.

I walked over to the grill and saw two types of sausage-shaped things rolling around on the revolving cooker. I could tell that one was a hot dog, but the other one was a mystery. I asked the girl behind the counter, "What is that?" and pointed to the unknown food item.

She didn't answer.

So I asked again. "What is that?" taking care to indicate exactly which revolving food I was curious about.

Again, no answer.

I tried a third time. And as if she'd just awoken, she responded slowly, "Cheeseburger."

I raised my eyebrows. "That thing?" I said.

"Cheeseburger," she said again, bored.

"You are going to stand there and tell me that tube of meat is a cheeseburger?"

She looked at the grill. Then back at me. Then

again at the grill. She exhaled heavy and long, then said, flatly, "Cheeseburger dog."

I ordered the hot dog.

I always remember that story when people ask about my enchanting new life as a famous person. It isn't all champagne and caviar. Sometimes it's cheeseburger dogs.

—

L.A. is a test for me. Will I let celebrity define me? Will I let it become who I am? Or will I remember where I am from, remember my purpose.

I don't want people waiting on me. It will be a sad day when I can't buy my own toilet paper. I think it is important to hold on to reality.

When it comes to Hollywood and my new life as a pop singer, I get weary of it, yes. But I didn't get here on my own. This opportunity was given to me. And I don't think it's my choice when it ends.

I believe all of this happened for a purpose, so I want my career to be purpose driven. I want my *life* to be purpose driven.

If I were to say I was done with it, I think that would be selfish. God gave me my voice for a much higher purpose than just to sing. I'm here for a reason. And if I decide that fame is a pain in my butt or that being chased down the street is scary, ultimately, that's inconsiderate.

In the end, I keep telling myself that this celebrity,

however moderate, has nothing to do with my wallet or my image. My purpose is to do good. And this is the form it has taken.

In church in Raleigh, the congregation used to say, "Make sure you use your voice for the Lord." I feel that is what I'm doing. And I will continue doing it until the Lord tells me to pipe down.

I had been looking for a church to join in Raleigh for some time. One morning I stopped by Leesville Baptist and I heard this kid singing. He had red hair and wire-rimmed glasses, but that voice. He couldn't have been more than thirteen. I joined the church after that.

—Frances Wilson, longtime family friend

CHAPTER EIGHTEEN

Make a Joyful Noise

I've always *thought* of myself as very open-minded. But I have since learned that I could stand to improve in that area.

Being open-minded was easy in Raleigh, where everyone is pretty much alike. I still consider myself tolerant, but until I moved out to L.A. I had never met an Orthodox Jew, or a Muslim, or an atheist or agnostic. I've always been very open to people who were not Christian, who had a different faith system. But atheists—that's a whole other ball of wax.

The first time I met such a person, my immediate reaction was No. No. No. No. No! You know? You're kidding me, right? What do you mean, none? No faith?

I don't get that. It's taken me some time to adjust to individuals who feel that way. I've never before known anybody who had *no* faith. I'm not sure how they get through the day.

It's tough for me to come to terms with the fact that some people don't believe anything. I can't see how that's even a possibility. I mean, I can understand people having different views, but *no* views? That's like not having an opinion on music. What do you mean, no opinion?

Obviously, I still have a way to go toward accepting their choices. But I do understand that faith is a choice.

—

My Aunt Dianne frequently sends me e-mails. The notes are heartfelt and inspirational. They are persistent reminders of the importance of relying on God. A recent letter asked, "Are you attending church or doing a study on your own? How is your walk with the Lord?" They are always signed, "Take care and have a Jesus Day."

However, in one recent submission Aunt Dianne shared that she was very unhappy that I chose to appear on Ellen DeGeneres's talk show. She felt that by doing her program I was condoning her lifestyle.

Sometimes I think Aunt Dianne worries about the wrong things.

—

I have attended Leesville Baptist Church since I was a toddler.

Leesville is a small, intimate church. The building is nondescript, brick and white cement, with a center front door. It sits at a crossroads with a shopping center and a strip mall and an empty field.

I went to this church every week for eighteen years. I was in the Bible school, the choir, and the youth group. I was a devoted member of the congregation in every way until high school.

When I was in high school I had a crisis of conscience. I began wrestling with my religion. I thought that maybe some of the messages it was passing down weren't the most Christian.

My faith in God and His direction in every person's life and in Jesus Christ and His life on earth and His death on the cross never wavered. What I questioned was the way it was presented.

This was the period of time when Southern Baptists were getting a bad rap for boycotting Teletubbies and Disney. It was really just laughable. You couldn't dance if you were a member of certain Baptist churches because they thought it was not appropriate. Women couldn't be ministers. One Baptist church in Raleigh would not marry a white man and a black woman. I remember thinking, *Are you kidding me?*

Then there was a church south of town that posted a neon sign every week that said things like "Twenty-nine people saved on Sunday!" Are we keeping score now?

Has church become McDonald's—billions and billions served?

So at age eighteen, after as many years, I stopped going to church.

—

A few years later I met some people who were Moravian. The Moravian church is a small, old, Protestant denomination that focuses on sharing God with people by showing His love.

My new friends explained that you don't necessarily have to talk about hellfire and brimstone, which is what the Baptist church was always about for me. You could communicate God's devotion to people and encourage them to follow that way. The faith was a lot less evangelical, a lot less rigid, and thus more inviting.

Unlike the Baptists, the Moravian church doesn't take positions on abortion or capital punishment. Moravians believe that those choices are up to the individual and depend on his or her relationship with God. They believe you get to heaven through Jesus Christ, who is God's son, and they accept all the traditional Protestant convictions. But the denomination is a lot less about telling people what they did wrong and more about praising people for what they did right.

I started going to this new church because I really liked the message. I was ready to join formally when the preacher at my old church left. He decided to quit kind of abruptly, and when I thought about it, I realized he'd been there as long as I had.

His departure reintroduced Leesville into my mind. I started looking back and apprehended that for a Southern Baptist preacher, he had been very open-minded. He wanted women to be in the church, and he was progressive about other social issues. I never really appreciated him until he left.

The more I thought about my old church, the more I missed the feeling of community. For better or worse, I had a history there.

This other church, the Moravian church, was lacking continuity for me. It didn't have that close-knit feeling of kinship. There were no Sunday picnics where you ate barbeque on the green. There were no potlucks with people telling stories about what I did when I was six or ten or fifteen years old. I missed that.

I decided to give Leesville Baptist another chance.

—

Today I am a proud Southern Baptist. But I still carry many of the Moravian ideas with me. I appreciate the idea of allowing people to have their own private walk with God. To me, God is about love, not condemnation.

It's healthy to go to church, but you can still be a Christian if you don't.

You can believe in God and not pray daily.

You can read the Bible on your own.

Faith is not about a building or a lifestyle. You can minister in many ways besides attending services or being a preacher. And I think that that's what I feel most thankful for—that I have the opportunity to minister now, in my own way.

—

Some people have argued that I'm too religious and that I talk about my faith too much. My response to them is that I'm not going to hide what I believe and what I think and how I feel, but I do my best not to shove it down anybody's throat. I'm not trying to change anybody's beliefs, but if someone asks me about it I'm happy to share it. I want to be here for that.

Other people have criticized me because I don't stand up for my beliefs enough. But my position is that there's a fine line that has to be walked. There are a lot of people who have given Christians a really bad name by being overly aggressive. Showing aggression and being judgmental turn people off and away from God.

—

It's very important to me that no one be offended by my performances.

I listen to the Christian radio station in my car, and if people ride in my car they might listen to it, too. Until recently, I've never been around people who said, "Turn that off, I don't want to hear it." And I have to question myself sometimes. Should I turn it off for them? Or should I keep it on for me?

Faith is not something I could ever give up on. I don't want to push anything in your face, but if you choose to look at religion and ask questions, I'm going to tell you what I think about it. I'm going to share what I believe without shame, but I'm going to strive to keep you from feeling uncomfortable or wrong about your own convictions. It's not my job to judge someone; it's not my job to mandate what someone else thinks or believes.

When I worked at the YMCA, I determined that the camp I ran would not sing songs that were unduly evangelical. We sang about God, but I didn't do overtly Christian songs because I had kids in there who were Jewish. Their parents had picked the Y because it was the best camp in town. It had the best programs and, in some regards, it was the cheapest. That's why they put their kids there. They didn't put their kids there to go to church.

The other camp faculty took issue with my not

singing about Jesus. Everybody disagreed with me. But I stood firm. I decided that no child was going to have a spiritual crisis on my watch.

—

Adults have a responsibility to children—all children, not just their own. You are always setting an example.

I was conscious of the fact that if I sang about Jesus to my kids at the Y, then some of the children might get confused. They looked up to me. They trusted me. I wasn't going to take advantage of that trust to advance my spiritual platform. Determing what faith a child will have is a decision that should be made at home, not at the YMCA camp.

—

Sometimes in my show I sing a song called "You Were There." It is an explicitly Christian song, and when I sing it the video screens show religious images.

When I tested my show for Disney—the tour sponsor—I was fully prepared for them to tell me that they wanted me to take the song out of the set. It's Disney, and I knew they might not want to endorse something with evangelical overtones. I think it's pretty subtle; it's a beautiful song and it lets people know who I am. But I was ready for Disney to tell me to lose it. And I was also ready to tell them to take their money back, because I wasn't prepared to edit out the song.

Disney was fine with "You Were There." But I still wrestle with my Christianity and how it fits into my new career. I wonder how much is too much? How much is not enough?

—

I want to make it very clear to people what I believe. I believe that Jesus is the son of God. I believe that people get to heaven through accepting Jesus as their personal savior, that he is the way to heaven and he is the way to God.

If other people choose to believe because I do, great. I want to show people God's love through what I do and who I am. At the same time, I don't feel I need to pass out Bibles at the concert.

I sing "You Were There" for me and for God. I'm happy if it makes people think. If people just want to enjoy the melody, that's fine, too. It's not an altar call.

I believe that Jesus is the way to heaven for me. He's the way that I'm getting there. But at the same time, I sincerely hope that people whom I love and care about who might be Jewish or Muslim or have different faiths and structure systems than I do also find peace in heaven. And I don't think it's my place to tell them they're not going to. Some people in my family may think so.

God never closes one door without opening another.

—Proverb quoted to Clayton throughout his childhood

CHAPTER NINETEEN

Keep Your Ears Open

M*y path through life* has taught me many things.

I know I am only at the beginning of my journey and there are many lessons still to come, but so far, so good.

My mother laid the foundation, showing me in word and deed what it means to be decent. She overcame every burden life presented her, and she did so with grace.

Though in my childhood I felt the emptiness of loss and the sting of regret, I was able to persevere thanks to the support of my family. I learned how strong the bond of brotherhood can be, even when it's under the surface, even when we are unable to speak about the contents of our hearts.

I learned that pride can make people foolish and that death comes but does not necessarily overcome.

I came to see how indispensable self-belief can be. How if you are unhappy with yourself, others will follow suit.

Once I found my voice, I was able to carve out an identity. I evolved into a person I could like and found that when I accepted my strengths and my limitations, I felt at peace.

As my mother said, "A man's reputation is only what men think him to be. His character is what God knows him to be."

In time, I had to learn what else I had to contribute besides singing. I needed to incorporate my individuality into a bigger world. I had to discover what more I had to offer of myself.

At the YMCA I found that making myself happy was a lot simpler when I concentrated on making other people happy. True joy comes from service, not from acquisition.

The time I spent teaching prepared me like nothing else for the life that was to come. Had I not learned the significance of making a difference in the world, the unexpected success that followed would have corrupted me.

Working with children with special needs ushered in a fresh selflessness. You cannot reside in ego when you work with kids. They demand so much, but they give back much more. They instill patience and gratitude for achievements great and small. Children teach you that you don't always get applause for your accomplishments; that any worthwhile validation comes from within.

The smallest good deed is better than the grandest intention.

I am profoundly grateful that my *American Idol* experience came on the heels of teaching because it allowed me to savor the joy of each moment. I was able to embrace my quirks and differences. I was proud of myself at last. I had found a way to be my authentic self.

I realized that performing is a high unto itself, but more important, it is a means to an end. Spreading happiness through song allowed me to lift people up, and that is a more meaningful purpose than anything as silly as seeking adulation.

There is no better exercise for strengthening the heart than reaching down and lifting people up. The Bubel/Aiken Foundation is the culmination of that realization. It is my purpose now. It is the why of me.

I know now that all of these events and epiphanies have resulted from provident direction. True happiness depends upon close alliance with God.

When I look back, the dots connect so clearly. It's hard to imagine that anything could have happened any differently.

He's more involved than most artists. He pays attention to every detail on every level. He is protective of his career. If I change one cue onstage, he asks me why it's different. Most artists wouldn't even notice. Clay knows what he wants. He has a vision. If he works as hard as he is working now, he'll be around forever.

—Chris Gratton, touring production manager
who has worked for the Pretenders, John Denver,
Natalie Cole, PJ Harvey, Limp Bizkit, and many others

CHAPTER TWENTY

When in Doubt, Hum

Whenever I am asked about what the future holds, I get a little nervous.

First, because it is not up to me. No earthly person knows the future. Not even Ms. Cleo.

Second, because it makes me think about the end, and I have so much I want to achieve before then. You know how people always say, "When it's my time, it's my time." And "I want you all to be happy for me when I'm gone."

Forget that. When I die I want everyone to be good and sad. I want there to be lots of tears. I want people to mourn for at least five years.

I'm kidding, of course. But seriously, I try not to

ponder the future because the last time I did that I ended up being acutely off track.

The future is not in my hands. There are, though, things I hope for.

World peace.

Equality.

Tolerance.

—

On less pensive days, I think I'd enjoy having a theme park.

I also imagine having my own talk show—a cross between Oprah's and Larry King's. It would be an issue show, not one that featured strippers on crack screaming at each other.

I guess I think about these avenues because I would love to find new ways to parlay any of my celebrity influence into something useful. I genuinely admire people who take all the sway they have and employ it not just to better their own world, but for the benefit of the wider world.

Who is to say that people will remember me? But if they do, then I plan to be remembered for having shared any success I was fortunate enough to experience with as many people as I could.

My absolute priority—more than having a hit song—is to set a good example. There is a difference between image and appearance. Your appearance is how you look. Your image comes from what you do. My goal is to be triumphant in using where I am to do something bigger than what I am.

—

Sometimes I ask myself: Why did this life happen to me?

I don't think anybody can answer that question. I don't know why I'm here doing what I'm doing—other than that it's a calling for me.

When I look back, I realize that God placed me into every situation that led me here. He introduced me into each one of those settings so that he could help shape me into a better servant. I didn't get this singing voice to make myself famous and rich. I got it to become a better messenger.

Remembering this is an ongoing project. I'm still working on making decisions that aren't geared just to help me. On not getting caught up in the paycheck and the people screaming my name. I'd like to think I'm there, but I'm not.

There are plenty of times when I need to sit myself down and redirect my intentions. I try to ask myself, *Whom will this serve?* If the only answer is *me*, then I should move on. Ego is a powerful foe. But so far, I think I'm winning.

—

I'm often asked what I would do to change the world if I had the power to do anything.

In my ideal world, no child would suffer. Charitable instincts would prevail. Those who could give, would give. There would be global acceptance of all different types of people. Society puts too much emphasis on what any category of person should be like—this is what a black male should act like, this is what an Asian female should act like, this is what a Frenchman should act like, this is what a Southerner should act like. Those stereotypes harm everyone. They are simplistic and reductive, and they need to go.

I wish that kids would be more accepting of each other, but that won't happen until adults are more accepting of each other, so that's probably a wish that's a long way from being fulfilled.

I hate to sound like a politician when I say this, but I'm tired of single mothers having to work three jobs to earn a poverty-level salary. I'm tired of kids not having somebody to look up to.

There are too many celebrities nowadays who pander to the lowest common denominator. I don't want my kids growing up thinking they should dress like so-and-so or talk like so-and-so in order to be cool or successful or rich or accepted.

More people need to understand that what they do or say affects not just them. Everyone has a right to state their opinion. But know that what you say and what you do affect people around you, whether you know them or not, whether they're in the room with you or in another country.

—

The thing about growing older is that you realize that everything your mother said to you was right. This is not always a painless epiphany. But in my case, it is a fact.

I may not have listened back then, but I listen more now. (Just don't tell her that.)

When I reflect now, I can see that all these lessons I learned in the last twenty-five years are truths my mother struggled to teach me. Eventually, I discovered them on my own, or from my friends and family. But Mom tried first. She knew all along.

Stop worrying about what other people think of you.

Be willing to take risks.

Failing doesn't hurt. Not trying does.

You can make an impression on someone without having to win.

Listen to your heart.

Stand up for what you believe in.

Keep on the sunny side of life.

Use your voice.

Make a joyful noise.

I used to get so enraged at my mom for telling me what to do and how to live.

I'd shout at her, "Mama, can't you be happy with

me as I am?" Of course, she was. But she realized that, at the time, I wasn't happy with me as I was.

—

Nobody is perfect. But we are all born with gifts.

I am just like every other single person in the world.

I have struggles.

I have satisfaction.

I have been abandoned.

I have been loved.

I have lost many more times than I have won.

What I've taken away from all of this—what I've finally come to understand—is that the greatest glory never comes from winning, but from rising each time you fall. A person is defined by what he chooses to do with his life, not by what happens to him.

—

I was lucky. My mother taught me to sing at a young age. She showed me that in every life there is music to be heard, if you only listen hard enough.

I believe that in every life there is a song to be sung.

Go.

Find your voice.

Then open up your mouth and set your song free.

Acknowledgments

Allison Glock, for sharing your amazing talents and making me sound smarter, nicer, and better than I could ever hope to be. I'm sure it was easy for you, because you are all of those things. Working with you is a joy and a pleasure.

Jonathan Karp and the folks at Random House, for sharing your talents and your vision, and for allowing me to tell my stories in a way that truly makes me proud.

Mom, Brett, Jeff, Amy, Granny, Papa, Nanny, and all of the family, whose strength and courage in allowing these stories to be told make me proud of where I come from, who I come from, who I am, and who I hope to be.

Additional thanks to Alan Nevins, Simon Renshaw, Jeff Rabhan, Marion Kraft, Nick Leisey, and Jess Rosen, for their tireless efforts toward making this project a success.

And to those many other individuals who have played such an important role in making me who I am by sharing of themselves in so many ways and thereby adding to the person I have become and am becoming.

Appendixes

—

Clayton Aiken Résumé

—

Date of Birth: 11-30-78

Height: 6'1"
Weight: 145
Hair: reddish blond
Eyes: green

VOCAL RANGE: TENOR

VOCAL EXPERIENCE

Carolina Hurricanes (NHL) hockey: Performer of national anthem
numerous times, 1998–2000.

North Carolina Music Connection, Benson, NC: Emcee and performer,
2001–June 2002.

Hometown Music Connection, Benson, NC: Emcee and performer,
1999, 2000, 2001 series, five shows a year.

Just by Chance and Friends, Dunn, NC: Cohost and performer, 1999,
2000, 2001 series, five shows a year.

Great American Gospelfest: First-place regional vocalist in Myrtle
Beach, SC, male category, fourth-place finals.

Garner Arts Association, Garner, NC: Showcase of stars, emcee and
performer, September 1998–September 1999, when show was
moved to Benson and changed to Hometown Music Connection.

Johnston Community College Country Showcase, Smithfield, NC:
Regular performer, 1998, 1999; guest performer, 2000.

Raleigh Ice Caps (ECHL): Frequent performer of national anthem,
1996–1997.

First-place winner, Johnston Community College Talent Search: 17-22
age category in 1996.

Pieces of Gold talent show (Wake County Public Schools): 1992,
1993, 1995, and 1996, with choral group (groups have to
audition).

Pieces of Gold solo act: 1997, required audition, with only two soloists selected.

DIRECTING EXPERIENCE

Best Little Christmas Pageant Ever, Garner Arts Association, 1998.

Best Little Christmas Pageant Ever, Southern Pines, NC, 1995, Assistant director; "100 Years of Broadway," assistant and performer.

ACTING EXPERIENCE

	Role	Play	Producing Group	Year
1.	Apple seller, ensemble	*Annie*	North Carolina Theatre Raleigh, NC	1997
2.	Leather apron painter	*1776*	North Carolina Theatre Raleigh, NC	1996
3.	Ewart Dunlop, quartet	*The Music Man*	Leesville Road High School Raleigh, NC	1996
4.	Confederate sniper	*Shenandoah*	North Carolina Theatre Raleigh, NC	1996
5.	Max	*The Best Little Christmas Pageant Ever*	Mannie's Dinner Theatre Southern Pines, NC	1995
6.	Townsperson, ensemble	*Cinderella*	Raleigh Little Theatre Raleigh, NC	1994, 1995, 1996
7.	Rolf Gruber	*The Sound of Music*	Mannie's Dinner Theatre Southern Pines, NC	1995
8.	Will Parker	*Oklahoma*	Leesville Road High School Raleigh, NC	1995

9.	Chorus	*Oliver*	Hull Ensemble Players	1992
			North Humberside,	
			Hull, England/Raleigh	

OTHER EXPERIENCES

Raleigh Boychoir: 2½ years, ages 11–13

North Carolina Junior All-State Chorus, 1993

Member numerous school choirs

Soloist, Fourth of July celebration, at North Carolina State Fairgrounds, 1995

Numerous high school and college beauty pageants

Host of Johnston County Beauty Pageant

From 2000 to 2002, I concentrated mostly on my education at the University of North Carolina—Charlotte, where I majored in special education. In between times, I hosted the Hometown Music Connection, which later became the North Carolina Music Connection. I also performed in and directed the show.

Favorite Childhood Recipes
—

GRANNY'S BEAN PIE

Clayton made this for his kids at the YMCA.

2	9-INCH PIE SHELLS
4	SLIGHTLY BEATEN EGGS
¼	CUP MELTED UNSALTED BUTTER
2	15-OUNCE CANS OF LIMA BEANS
⅓	CUP EVAPORATED MILK
1	TEASPOON CINNAMON
1	TEASPOON BAKING SODA
2	CUPS OF SUGAR
1	TEASPOON VANILLA

1. Bake the pie shells and cool.
2. Using an electric blender, mix the eggs, butter, beans, milk, cinnamon, and baking soda on medium speed for 2 minutes.
3. Pour the mixture into a bowl and add the sugar and vanilla. Mix well.
4. Pour into the pie shells. Bake at 350°F for 1 hour until golden brown. Makes two pies.

CHERRY YUM YUM

1 ½ STICKS MARGARINE

3 CUPS GRAHAM CRACKER CRUMBS

2 PACKAGES DREAM WHIP

1 CUP COLD MILK

1 8-OUNCE PACKAGE CREAM CHEESE

¾ CUP SUGAR

2 CANS CHERRY PIE FILLING

1. Melt the margarine and mix with the graham crackers. Put half on the bottom of a trifle bowl.
2. Mix the Dream Whip and milk till fluffy. Beat in the cream cheese a little at a time. Alternate with the sugar.
3. Pour half the cream cheese mixture over the crumbs. Then pour on the two cans of pie filling. Add the rest of the cream cheese mixture and top with graham crackers.

CLAYTON'S FAVORITE SPAGHETTI SAUCE

3 POUNDS GROUND BEEF

I LARGE ONION, MINCED

I LARGE CAN CRUSHED TOMATOES

I LARGE CAN TOMATO PUREE

I LARGE CAN TOMATO PASTE

DASH GARLIC SALT

I TEASPOON MINCED GARLIC

I LARGE BAY LEAF

BASIL, OREGANO, SALT, PEPPER, SUGAR TO TASTE

1. Brown the beef and onion in a large skillet. Drain.
2. Combine the remaining ingredients in a large pot. Let it boil. Turn down the heat; add the beef and onion. Simmer as long as you can.

FYI: *Clayton does not like mushrooms or bell peppers.*

CUBE STEAK AND GRAVY

FLOUR

SALT AND PEPPER

CUBE STEAK

1. Mix the flour, salt, and pepper together.
2. Run water over the steak. Roll it in the flour mixture.
3. Panfry the steak in ½ inch of cooking oil until done.
4. I have no recipe for gravy. It is a trial-and-error process, and I made a lot of lumpy gravy before I got it right. So don't give up.
5. Using drippings from the pan, sprinkle in flour and stir to make a soft, runny paste. Let the paste brown in the pan to the desired color, then pour cold water in, a little at a time, stirring constantly. With a lot of practice you will get it right. It is the salt and pepper that make it good. So add lots, to taste, and watch your blood pressure.

Open Letter from Faye to Clayton

—

Dear Son,

From the day you were born I knew something special would happen in your life.

You were so wise beyond your years. I could not predict the future but only knew that God had given you a special voice for some reason.

I know life was not easy sometimes but God never said it would be. He said only to have faith in Him.

The road traveled was a little rough but we endured the storm. You have achieved more than my wildest dreams in your short life.

Never regret the past but learn from it.

Don't lose sight of your dreams, for as long as you dream, there is hope.

Keep believing in yourself. If you do, so will everyone else. Remember, you have the ability to accomplish anything you wish, but never do so at others' expense.

Love others and as you do, that love will return to you.

I am so proud of the young man you have become. I remember we used to sing, "You can't be a beacon if your light don't shine."

Yours is shining bright now and others look up to you as a role model.

Don't let that be a burden but carry that trust with you. Enjoy this time and make the most of it.

I love you with all my heart.

Carry on with honesty, confidence, and pride.

Remember when you feel alone that I am always by your side.

Always with Love,
Mom

P.S. I HOPE YOU DANCE.

CLAY AIKEN was one of the two finalists in the 2003 *American Idol* season, and is undoubtedly the biggest star to emerge from that hit show. Aiken's debut album, *Measure of a Man,* entered the *Billboard* 200 at number 1 in October 2003, selling 612,000 copies during its first week. Aiken's single "This Is the Night"/"Bridge Over Troubled Water" won the 2003 *Billboard* Music Award for Bestselling Single. He was honored as the Fan's Choice winner at the 2003 American Music Awards. Also in 2003, *People* magazine named the North Carolina crooner one of its Top Entertainers of the Year and one of its Sexiest Men Alive. And in another testament to Aiken's immense popularity, he earned *TV Guide*'s Fan's Favorite Reality Star of 2003.

For more information, visit www.clayaiken.com.

ALLISON GLOCK is the author of *Beauty Before Comfort,* an acclaimed memoir about life in West Virginia, now available from Random House Trade Paperbacks. She has written articles for many magazines, including *GQ* and *The New York Times Magazine.* She lives in Knoxville, Tennessee.